500 Chicken

Recipes

igloobooks

Published in 2016
by Igloo Books Ltd
Cottage Farm
Sywell
Northants
NN6 0BJ
www.igloobooks.com

Food photography and recipe development: PhotoCuisine UK
Front and back cover images © PhotoCuisine UK

HUN001 0916
6 8 10 9 7 5
ISBN: 978-1-78343-220-2

Printed and manufactured in China

CONTENTS

LIGHT BITES & STARTERS

SERVES 6–8

Thai Vermicelli Soup

PREPARATION TIME 30 MINUTES

COOKING TIME 40–45 MINUTES

INGREDIENTS

3 tbsp vegetable oil
4 spring onions (scallions), sliced
1 red pepper, deseeded and diced
2 cloves of garlic, finely chopped
1 red chilli (chili), finely sliced
2 stalks lemongrass, bruised
1 tbsp fresh ginger, grated
1 tsp turmeric
3–4 chicken breasts, skinned and finely chopped
2 tsp tamarind paste
2 tbsp fish sauce
400 ml / 14 fl. oz / 1 ½ cups coconut milk
200 ml / 7 fl. oz / ¾ cup chicken stock
150 g / 5 oz / ⅔ cup vermicelli noodles
1–2 limes, juiced
½ bunch coriander (cilantro), finely chopped, stalks reserved

- Heat the oil in a wok or large pan and fry the onion and pepper until deep gold and sweet. Add the garlic and chilli and cook for 2 minutes. Add the cubed chicken, lemongrass, ginger and turmeric and allow to colour on all sides.
- Stir in the tamarind and fish sauce, then pour over the coconut milk and chicken stock and add the coriander stalks. Lower the heat and leave to simmer for 15–20 minutes until the chicken is cooked through, adding the noodles for the last 5–8 minutes of cooking.
- Adjust the seasoning and stir in the lime juice and chopped coriander just before serving in deep warmed bowls.

Spicy Thai Soup

- Add a pinch of chilli (chili) flakes for an extra kick.

SERVES 4

Chicken with Figs and Broad Beans

PREPARATION TIME 15 MINUTES

COOKING TIME 30 MINUTES

INGREDIENTS

2 tbsp olive oil
4 chicken thighs, skinned
1 onion, peeled and finely chopped
400 g / 14 oz / 1 ½ cups chopped tomatoes
2 sprigs basil leaves
salt and pepper
4 quartered, ripe figs
100 g / 3 ½ oz / ½ cup broad beans

- Heat the olive oil in a pan and cook the chicken thighs until golden on all sides. Remove and set aside.
- Add the onion and cook until softened, then add the tomatoes, basil and a little seasoning. Return the thighs to the pan, cover, and simmer until thickened and the chicken is cooked through.
- Meanwhile blanch the broad beans and pod them, discarding the grey skins.
- Just before serving add the figs and broad beans to the sauce to heat through.

Chicken with Figs and Peas

- Fresh peas make a nice substitute for the beans.

SERVES 4–6 · 5

Chicken Curry Filo Parcels

- Preheat the oven to 200°C (180°C fan) / 400F / gas 6.
- Heat the oil in a pan and sauté the onion for about 10 minutes or until golden-brown. Add the garlic and ginger and fry for another minute.
- Add the spices and stir well, then add 200 ml water and the chicken and cook gently for 10 minutes or so. Once the liquid has mostly evaporated, stir in just enough yoghurt to bind and leave to cool.
- Keeping the remaining filo sheets covered with a damp tea towel, remove one at a time from the pack and brush with melted butter before using.
- Place 2 sheets of pastry on a surface, brush each with melted butter, then spoon a little of the chicken mixture into the middle. Wrap the pastry around to enclose the filling. Repeat until all the filling and pastry is used up.
- Brush the tops with a little egg yolk, then bake in the oven for 15–20 minutes.

Chicken Curry Parcels with Sauce · 6

- Serve alongside garlic mayonnaise.

PREPARATION TIME 25 MINUTES

COOKING TIME 45 MINUTES

INGREDIENTS

3 tbsp vegetable oil
1 onion, peeled and finely sliced
2 cloves of garlic, chopped
1 tsp fresh ginger, grated
1 tsp ground coriander (cilantro)
½ tsp turmeric
1 tsp ground cumin
1 tbsp garam masala
1 tsp paprika
4 chicken thighs, skinned, deboned and diced
2–3 tbsp plain yoghurt
12–16 sheets filo pastry
120 g / 4 oz / ½ cup butter, melted
1 egg yolk, beaten

SERVES 2 · 7

Artichoke and Chicken Salad

- Slice the chicken and place in a salad bowl with the artichoke hearts and tomatoes.
- Whisk together the mustard and vinegar, then whisk in the oil until emulsified. Add 1 tbsp artichoke oil if available. Season.
- Toss the salad ingredients in the dressing, sprinkle with chopped chives and serve.

Warm Artichoke Salad · 8

- Sauté the artichoke hearts in a little oil with the chicken, then toss while still warm with the tomatoes and dressing and serve on thick toast.

PREPARATION TIME 15 MINUTES

INGREDIENTS

2 chicken breasts, cooked
250 g / 9 oz / 1 cup prepared globe artichoke hearts, drained of oil, halved or quartered
2 tomatoes, cored and diced
1 tbsp Dijon mustard
1 tbsp red wine vinegar
3 tbsp extra virgin olive oil
salt and pepper
10 chive stems, chopped

9

SERVES 4

Chicken Bites with Fresh Mint

Spicy Chicken Bites 10

- Add a pinch of dried chilli (chili) flakes for an extra kick.

Tarragon Chicken Bites 11

- Use fresh tarragon leaves in place of the mint.

PREPARATION TIME 5 MINUTES
+ MARINATING TIME

COOKING TIME 10 MINUTES

....

INGREDIENTS

4 chicken breasts, skinned and cubed
150 ml / 5 fl. oz / ⅔ cup plain yoghurt
1 bunch mint leaves, finely chopped
salt and pepper
½ lemon, juiced
½ cucumber, finely sliced
4 pitta breads

- Toss the chicken in the yoghurt and mint and leave to marinate in the refrigerator for about 20–30 minutes.
- Heat a griddle or frying pan until hot, then wipe off any excess marinade and cook the chicken until sizzling and golden.
- Season and drizzle with lemon juice, then serve with cucumber and warmed pitta breads.

12

SERVES 4

Chicken Courgette Kebabs

- Thread the chicken, onion chunks and courgette slices alternately onto soaked wooden skewers.
- Drizzle with oil and griddle over medium heat for 10–12 minutes until golden and cooked through.
- Season well, scatter with tarragon and squeeze over a little lemon juice before serving.

PREPARATION TIME 10 MINUTES

COOKING TIME 10–12 MINUTES

INGREDIENTS

2 large chicken breasts
½ red onion, peeled and cut into chunks
½ courgette (zucchini), thickly sliced
2 tbsp olive oil
a few fresh tarragon leaves, torn
½ lemon, juiced
salt and pepper

Turkey Courgette Kebabs   **13**

- Try using turkey breast meat for a change, but marinate in olive oil and oregano for 30 minutes before cooking to add flavour.

14

SERVES 2

Chicken and Pickled Salad Bagels

- Thickly slice the chicken and set aside.
- Toss the carrot and courgette with the vinegar, sugar and salt and leave to marinate for 5–10 minutes, until still crunchy but starting to soften.
- Toast the bagels.
- Place lettuce leaves on the bottom bagel halves, top with drained pickled vegetables then the sliced chicken and the other bagel half on top.

PREPARATION TIME 20 MINUTES

INGREDIENTS

2 chicken breasts, skin on, cooked
1 carrot, peeled and cut into matchsticks
1 courgette (zucchini), peeled and cut into matchsticks
2 tbsp rice vinegar
1 tbsp sugar
1 tsp salt
4 lettuce leaves
2–4 bagels, depending on appetite

Chicken and Pickled Salad Pittas   **15**

- Substitute the bagels for pittas instead.

16

SERVES 4

Colombo Style Chicken Legs

PREPARATION TIME 40 MINUTES
+ MARINATING TIME

COOKING TIME 25–30 MINUTES

....

INGREDIENTS

1 tbsp vegetable oil
1 onion, peeled and chopped
3 cloves of garlic, crushed
2 tbsp curry powder
6 sprigs thyme leaves
1 tsp ground allspice
½ tsp ground cinnamon
2 bay leaves
1-2 Scotch Bonnet chillies (chilies)
8 spring onions (scallions), ends
trimmed
500 ml / 1 pint / 2 cups chicken stock
400 g / 14 oz / 1 ½ cups canned
chopped tomatoes
4 chicken legs

- Heat the oil in a large pan and cook the onion and garlic with the spices until softened.
- Add the chillies and spring onions, chicken stock and tomatoes and simmer for 30 minutes or until thick and reduced.
- Leave to cool, then coat the chicken thoroughly in the marinade and leave for 4 hours or overnight.
- Preheat the oven to 190°C (170°C fan) / 375F / gas 5.
- Sit the chicken in a roasting tin and cook in the oven for 25–30 minutes until cooked through.
- Meanwhile simmer any excess marinade to serve alongside.
- Serve the chicken with the sauce.

Colombo Style Chicken Wings

17

- Substitute the chicken legs for chicken wings.

18

SERVES 4

Chicken Tandoori Tomato Salad

PREPARATION TIME 10 MINUTES
+ MARINATING TIME

COOKING TIME 15 MINUTES

....

INGREDIENTS

4 skinless chicken breasts,
diced evenly
1 tbsp vegetable oil
400 g / 14 oz / 1 ½ cups baby
spinach leaves
3 tbsp capers, drained

FOR THE MARINADE
1 tsp ground cumin
1 tsp ground coriander (cilantro)
1 tsp garam masala
1 tsp ground cinnamon
1 ½ tsp tandoori chilli (chili) powder
1 tsp paprika
1 tsp caster (superfine) sugar
1 clove garlic, minced
salt and pepper
300 ml / 10 fl. oz / 1 ¼ cups canned
tomatoes

- Prepare the tandoori marinade by mixing together all the ingredients for the marinade apart from the tomatoes in a mixing bowl. Add the chicken, mix well, then cover and chill for at least 1 hour.
- Shake off any excess and fry the chicken briskly in the oil until golden and cooked through.
- Meanwhile pour the tomatoes into a pan with the excess marinade and simmer for 10 minutes until thickened.
- Serve the chicken and sauce spooned over baby spinach leaves and topped with the capers.

Tandoori Chicken with Rice

19

- Stir the spinach into warm rice, then serve alongside the chicken for a more substantial meal. Reduce the cooking time by 10 minutes.

20

SERVES 6–8

Chicken and Pistachio Pâté

- Heat the chicken stock in a pan and poach the chicken for 10 minutes until cooked. Remove with a slotted spoon and leave to cool.
- Whisk the gelatine into the hot stock until dissolved.
- Fill a terrine mould with the chicken, scattering over the pistachios and seasoning as you go.
- Pour the liquid over the chicken and refrigerate for at least 4 hours until set.
- Serve in thick slices with sun-dried tomatoes and salad.

PREPARATION TIME 30 MINUTES

COOKING TIME 30 MINUTES

INGREDIENTS

500 g / 1 lb / 2 cups chicken breast, skinned and cut into chunks
400 ml / 14 fl. oz / 1 ½ cups chicken stock
100 g / 3 ½ oz / ½ cup pistachios, chopped
2 leaves gelatine, soaked in cold water
salt and pepper
sun-dried tomatoes and salad leaves to serve

Chinese Flavoured Pâté

21

- Try using cashew nuts and 2 tbsp soy sauce and 1 star anise in the chicken stock to give a tiny hint of Eastern flavours.

22

SERVES 4

Tunisian Salad

- Preheat the oven to 220°C (200°C fan) / 425F / gas 7.
- Place the peppers in a snug roasting tin and drizzle with oil. Roast for 40–45 minutes until blackened. When cooked, place in a freezer bag to cool.
- Cook the potatoes in boiling salted water until tender to the point of a knife. Drain thoroughly.
- Rub the harissa into the chicken on all sides and roast in the oven alongside the peppers for 20 minutes until cooked through.
- When the peppers have cooled enough to handle, peel away the skins to leave the soft flesh and chop roughly. Tip into a large serving bowl with the olives, tomatoes, onion and drizzle over extra virgin oil, lemon juice and seasoning. Add the potatoes and toss gently.
- Slice the chicken and place on top of the salad before serving.

PREPARATION TIME 20 MINUTES

COOKING TIME 45 MINUTES

INGREDIENTS

2 red peppers, deseeded and halved
2 tbsp olive oil
500 g / 1 lb / 2 cups new potatoes, halved
salt
2 chicken breasts, skin on
2 tbsp harissa paste
60 g / 2 oz / ¼ cup black olives
12 cherry tomatoes, halved
½ red onion, finely chopped
2 tbsp extra virgin olive oil
½ lemon, juiced

Tunisian Salad with Eggs

23

- Quartered hard boiled eggs would make a good addition to this salad.

24

SERVES 4

Chicken Satay with Coconut Shavings

PREPARATION TIME 15 MINUTES

COOKING TIME 10 MINUTES

....

INGREDIENTS

8 chicken thighs, skinned, deboned
and cut in half
½ coconut
1 lime, juiced

FOR THE MARINADE/SAUCE
2 shallots, peeled and finely chopped
½–1 red chilli (chili), finely chopped
2 cloves of garlic, finely chopped
1 cm piece fresh ginger, grated
5 tbsp peanut butter
1 tbsp tamarind paste
2 tbsp soy sauce
100 ml / 3 ½ fl. oz / ½ cup coconut
milk
1 tsp palm or dark brown sugar
1 tbsp fish sauce

- Mix together the marinade ingredients and pour half over the chicken pieces.
- Leave to marinate for at least 4 hours or overnight.
- Skewer the chicken onto soaked wooden kebab sticks. Griddle over a high heat until blackened in patches and cooked through, about 6–8 minutes.
- Meanwhile heat the remaining sauce in a small pan, then squeeze in a little lime juice.
- Carve out shavings of fresh coconut, being very careful with your fingers.
- Serve the chicken sprinkled with fresh coconut and any sauce alongside.

Satay Chicken Rolled in Coconut **25**

- If you can't source fresh coconut, roll the cooked chicken in desiccated coconut for an extra dimension.

26

SERVES 2

Chicken on Toast with Bearnaise

PREPARATION TIME 15 MINUTES

COOKING TIME 30 MINUTES

....

INGREDIENTS

1 tbsp tarragon, chopped
1 shallot, finely chopped
6 black peppercorns, crushed
2 tbsp white wine vinegar
150 ml / 5 fl. oz / ⅔ cup dry white
wine
3 egg yolks
1 tsp mustard powder
25 g / 1 oz butter at room
temperature
180 g / 6 oz / ¾ cup butter, melted
salt and pepper
1 chicken breast, skin on
2 thick slices sourdough bread,
toasted
½ red onion, thinly sliced and tossed
with 1 tbsp white wine vinegar
vegetable oil

- Make the bearnaise: Put the tarragon, shallot, peppercorns, vinegar and wine in a pan and reduce by a third. Strain.
- Whisk the egg yolks and mustard together in a bowl over a pan of barely simmering water.
- Whisk in the vinegar reduction, add a tbsp water.
- Beat in the 25 g butter a little at a time, then slowly trickle in the melted butter a drop at a time, continually whisking, until the sauce has emulsified and thickened. Season and keep warm until needed.
- Meanwhile heat a griddle pan until smoking. Rub the chicken with a little oil, season and cook skin-side down on the griddle pan until golden. Turn over and cook on the other side until cooked through.
- Slice the chicken in half and arrange on the toast. Top with the pickled onion and spoon over the warm bearnaise.

Griddled Chicken with Aioli **27**

- This would work well with a home-made garlic mayonnaise, or just stir crushed garlic into prepared French-style mayo.

28

SERVES 4

Thyme Chicken with Rose Wine

Lavender Chicken

29

- Take this one stage further in summer and substitute the coriander seeds for lavender heads before barbecuing the chicken.

Chicken in White Wine

30

- If it's not quite summery enough, use white wine instead of rose wine.

PREPARATION TIME 10 MINUTES
+ MARINATING TIME

COOKING TIME 20 MINUTES

....

INGREDIENTS

4 chicken breasts
100 ml / 3 ½ fl. oz / ½ cup rose wine
4 sprigs thyme leaves
1 tbsp coriander (cilantro) seeds, lightly crushed
salt and pepper
2 tbsp olive oil
1 cos lettuce
1 tbsp red wine vinegar
2 tbsp extra virgin olive oil

- Marinate the chicken in the wine, thyme, coriander and a little seasoning for at least 30 minutes.
- Preheat the oven to 190°C (170°C fan) / 375F / gas 5.
- Sit the chicken in a roasting tin, drizzle with a little oil and roast for 20 minutes or until just cooked through. Set aside to rest.
- Tear the cos lettuce into separate leaves. Whisk the red wine vinegar with the extra virgin oil and a little seasoning and lightly coat the lettuce.
- Thickly slice the chicken and serve on top of the lettuce.

31

SERVES 4

Spanish Chicken with Pearl Barley Risotto

Chicken and Tomato Rolls

32

- You can use diced tomato in place of or in addition to the red pepper for a fresher flavour.

Chicken with Serrano Ham

33

- Layer on a slice of Serrano ham for a smoky flavour.

PREPARATION TIME 20 MINUTES

COOKING TIME 40 MINUTES

....

INGREDIENTS

4 chicken escalopes
2 tbsp olive oil
1 red pepper, deseeded and very finely diced
1 clove of garlic, crushed
200 g / 7 oz / ¾ cup cream cheese
8 slices chorizo
salt and pepper
1 onion, peeled and finely chopped
30 g / 1 oz butter
150 g / 5 oz / ⅔ cup pearl barley
100 ml / 3 ½ fl. oz / ½ cup dry white wine
400 ml / 14 fl. oz / 1 ½ cups chicken stock
½ lemon, zested

- Preheat the oven to 180°C (160°C fan) / 350F / gas 4.
- Place the chicken between 2 pieces of cling film and use a saucepan to flatten out to about 1 cm (½ in) thick.
- Sauté the peppers and garlic in a little oil until tender then leave to cool. Mix with the cream cheese.
- Spread the cream cheese mix evenly over the chicken escalopes then top with 2 slices chorizo and roll into a sausage shape. Secure with toothpicks if necessary. Roast in the oven for about 15–20 minutes until cooked through, then set aside to rest.
- Meanwhile sweat the onion in the butter, then add the barley. Stir in the white wine, simmer for 5 minutes, then add the chicken stock, Stir well, then simmer for about 20–30 minutes or until the barley is tender and the stock mostly absorbed. Season and add the lemon juice.
- Slice the chicken in half and serve with the risotto alongside.

34

SERVES 2

Thai Chicken and Pear Noodles

- Heat the oils in a wok and stir fry the chicken until golden.
- Add the pears and cook briefly. Whisk together the dressing, pour into the wok and toss to coat.
- Cook the rice noodles according to packet instructions, then drain thoroughly.
- Toss the noodles and beansprouts in the wok and reheat briefly, then serve in deep bowls, scattered with fresh coriander.

PREPARATION TIME 10 MINUTES

COOKING TIME 10–15 MINUTES

INGREDIENTS

1 tbsp vegetable oil
1 tsp sesame oil
2 chicken thighs, skinned, deboned and chopped
2 ripe pears, peeled, cored and chopped
200 g / 7 oz / ¾ cup rice noodles
60 g / 2 oz / ½ cup beansprouts
fresh coriander (cilantro) leaves, to garnish

FOR THE DRESSING
60 ml / 2 fl. oz / ¼ cup soy sauce
juice and zest of 1 lime
1 red chilli (chili), finely chopped
1 tsp tamarind paste
2 tsp soft brown sugar

Thai Chicken Noodles
with Pineapple

 35

- Chunks of refreshing pineapple would make a good foil to the sweet-sharp dressing.

36

SERVES 2

Chicken and Bacon Pancakes

- Heat the oil in a pan and sauté the chicken and bacon until golden.
- Lay out the pancakes on the surface and spoon over the meat, then top with a few spinach leaves. Roll up into sausage shapes and set aside.
- Heat the coconut milk in a small pan and simmer with the spring onions and coriander for 5 minutes. Season with the soy sauce.
- Spoon onto a plate and set the pancakes on top. Garnish with fresh chive stalks.

PREPARATION TIME 15 MINUTES

COOKING TIME 10 MINUTES

INGREDIENTS

2 tbsp olive oil
2 chicken breasts, skinned and cubed
4 rashers streaky bacon, chopped
handful baby spinach leaves
2 pancakes, ready-made
3 spring onions (scallions), finely chopped
¼ bunch fresh coriander (cilantro) chopped
150 ml / 5 fl. oz / ⅔ cup coconut milk
1 tbsp soy sauce
fresh chives to garnish

Chicken and Prawn Pancakes

 37

- Substitute the bacon for cooked large prawns.

38

SERVES 4

Glazed Chicken Wings

PREPARATION TIME 10 MINUTES

COOKING TIME 30–40 MINUTES

INGREDIENTS

12–16 chicken wings
2 tbsp soy sauce
1 tbsp paprika
1 tsp cayenne pepper
2–3 tbsp runny honey
salt and pepper
250 g / 9 oz / 1 cup basmati rice
½ head broccoli, separated into very
small florets
1 carrot, peeled and diced
2 tbsp sesame seeds, toasted

- Preheat the oven to 180°C (160°C fan) / 350F / gas 4.
- Tip the wings into a foil-lined roasting tin. Mix together the soy sauce, paprika, cayenne and honey – you may want more soy, honey or spice. Pour over the wings and coat thoroughly. Roast in the oven for 30–40 minutes until sticky and cooked.
- Meanwhile cook the rice in boiling salted water according to packet instructions. 3 minutes before the end of cooking time, add the broccoli and carrots to the pan to cook.
- When the rice is tender, drain thoroughly and leave to steam dry.
- Sprinkle the cooked wings with sesame seeds and serve with the rice.

Chicken Wings with Honey Mustard Glaze

39

- Add 1 large tbsp of grain mustard to the glaze for a punch.

40

SERVES 4

Chicken Satay Brochettes

PREPARATION TIME 15 MINUTES

COOKING TIME 10 MINUTES

INGREDIENTS

8 chicken thighs, boned and skinned
½ red chilli (chili), finely chopped
2 cloves of garlic, finely chopped
1 cm piece fresh ginger, grated
5 tbsp peanut butter
2 tbsp soy sauce
1 tsp palm or dark brown sugar
1 tbsp fish sauce
1 lime, juiced
1 carrot, peeled
1 courgette (zucchini)
2 peppers, deseeded and finely sliced
1 tbsp rice vinegar
1 tbsp sugar
salt and pepper

- Halve the chicken pieces.
- Mix together the chilli, garlic, ginger, peanut butter, soy sauce, sugar, fish sauce, and lime juice. Pour over the chicken pieces.
- Leave to marinate for at least 4 hours or overnight.
- Meanwhile, use a vegetable peeler to cut the carrot and courgette into ribbons and mix with the peppers. Toss with the vinegar, sugar and salt and leave to lightly pickle.
- Thread the chicken pieces onto soaked wooden skewers.
- Griddle over a high heat until blackened in patches and cooked through, about 6–8 minutes.
- Serve with the pickled vegetables alongside.

Chicken Satay with Rice

41

- Serve the skewers on a bed of boiled rice.

SERVES 4
42

Chicken and Pepper Kebabs

- Toss the chicken chunks with oregano, oil, a little lemon juice and seasoning. Leave to marinate for 20 minutes.
- Thread the chicken onto soaked wooden skewers alternating with the peppers and onion. Add the halved garlic cloves in between the chicken and peppers for extra flavour.
- Grill or griddle until the chicken is golden and just cooked through, about 8–10 minutes.
- Serve with lemon juice squeezed over and a little more salt. Remove the garlic before eating.

PREPARATION TIME 30 MINUTES

COOKING TIME 10 MINUTES

INGREDIENTS

4 chicken breasts, skinned and cut into chunks
1 tsp dried oregano
4 tbsp olive oil
½ lemon, juiced
salt and pepper
1 green pepper, deseeded and roughly chopped
1 red pepper, deseeded and roughly chopped
1 onion, roughly chopped
4 garlic cloves, skin on, halved

Chicken Pepper Pittas
43

- Warmed split pitta breads filled with the chicken, peppers and a good dollop of garlic mayo are great for parties.

SERVES 4
44

Chicken, Almond and Coconut Brochettes

- Marinate the chicken in the coconut milk, chilli, fish sauce and a third of the lime juice for at least 30 minutes.
- Thread onto skewers and barbecue or griddle until cooked, about 8 minutes. Once cooked, roll in the ground almonds.
- Meanwhile whiz the mangos in a liquidiser with the remaining lime juice and a little water to make a smooth sauce.
- Decant into a bowl and sprinkle with a little sea salt. Serve alongside the chicken.

PREPARATION TIME 20 MINUTES

COOKING TIME 8–10 MINUTES

INGREDIENTS

4 chicken breasts, skinned and cut into strips
150 ml / 5 fl. oz / ⅔ cup coconut milk
1 red chilli (chili), chopped
1–1 ½ limes, juiced
1 tbsp fish sauce
2 tbsp ground almonds
2 mangos, halved, stoned and peeled
sea salt

Chicken Pistachio Coconut Skewers
45

- For extra colour and flavour, roll in finely chopped pistachios.

46

SERVES 2

Lemon Chicken Salad

PREPARATION TIME 15 MINUTES

INGREDIENTS

2 chicken breasts, cooked
2 preserved lemons, chopped
1 tbsp capers, drained
2 tomatoes, cored and chopped
½ bunch parsley, chopped
small handful sorrel leaves
400 g / 14 oz / 1 ½ cups canned
chickpeas, drained
2 tbsp roasted peanuts, chopped
salt and pepper
3 tbsp extra virgin olive oil

- Shred the chicken breasts and add to a bowl. Add the lemons, capers, tomatoes, sorrel, parsley, chickpeas and peanuts, and toss to combine.
- Add the oil and season generously and toss, then serve.

Warm Lemon Chicken Salad

47

- Add the salad to a pan, minus the sorrel leaves, and warm gently. Then serve with the sorrel leaves scattered over.

48

MAKES 12

Chicken, Cheese and Herb Empanadas

PREPARATION TIME 40 MINUTES

COOKING TIME 15 MINUTES

INGREDIENTS

350 g / 12 oz / 1 ½ cups plain
(all purpose) flour
pinch salt
¼ tsp baking powder
180 g / 6 oz / ¾ cup butter, melted
2 eggs

FOR THE FILLING

2 tbsp olive oil
1 onion, peeled and finely chopped
1 clove of garlic, finely chopped
1 pepper, deseeded and chopped
1 tsp smoked paprika
1 tsp ground cumin
150 g / 5 oz / ⅔ cup mild cheese,
grated
200 g / 7 oz / ¾ cup chicken breast,
cooked and diced
1 bunch parsley, finely chopped
salt and pepper
1–2 tbsp sesame seeds

- Preheat the oven to 200°C (180°C fan) / 400F / gas 6.
- Sieve the flour, salt and baking powder into a bowl and mix in the melted butter and 1 egg, beaten. Gradually stir in 100 ml warm water to make a soft dough. Wrap in cling film and chill for 30 minutes.
- Heat the oil in a pan and sweat the onion until softened. Add the garlic and pepper and cook until softened.
- Add the spices, chicken and a splash of water and cook until hot, season and set aside to cool.
- Roll the pastry out to 3 mm thickness and cut out 24 circles around 6 cm (2 ½ in) in diameter. Spoon the chicken filling onto half the circles and scatter the cheese and herbs over the top.
- Place the remaining pastry circles on top and pinch the edges to seal.
- Brush with the remaining egg, sprinkle with sesame seeds and bake in the oven for about 15 minutes.

Spicy Chicken Vegetable Empanadas

49

- Use 1 aubergine, diced and 1 finely chopped red chilli in place of the cheese.

50

SERVES 2

Chicken and Avocado Salad

Chicken Avocado Salad with Chicory **51**

- Leaves of chicory would go well with orange, adding a bitter crunch.

Chicken Avocado Salad with Fennel **52**

- Add thinly sliced fennel for freshness.

PREPARATION TIME 10 MINUTES

COOKING TIME 20 MINUTES

INGREDIENTS

2 chicken breasts
1 tbsp olive oil
salt and pepper
1 tsp paprika
1–2 avocadoes, halved and stoned
1 large orange
½ red onion, peeled and finely sliced into half moons
2 tbsp extra virgin olive oil

- Preheat the oven to 200°C (180°C fan) / 400F / gas 6.
- Drizzle the chicken with oil, sprinkle with seasoning and paprika and roast for 20 minutes. Leave to rest.
- Chop the avocadoes and tip into a bowl. Peel the orange rind off with a knife, slicing it off to reveal the segments. Cut the segments out of the orange, slicing either side of the white pith, over the bowl to catch any juice. Add the segments to the bowl with the red onion and extra virgin oil and toss gently.
- Spoon carefully onto a plate, slice the chicken and sit on top of the salad. Sprinkle with extra paprika.

53

SERVES 4

Chicken Brochettes with Peach Chutney

PREPARATION TIME 15 MINUTES

COOKING TIME 15 MINUTES

INGREDIENTS

4 chicken breasts, skinned and cut into bite-size pieces
2 tbsp olive oil
1 tsp ground cumin
1 tsp ground coriander (cilantro)
5 peaches, halved and stoned
½ tbsp sugar
6 tbsp extra virgin olive oil
½ red chilli (chili), finely chopped (optional)

- Preheat the oven to 200°C (180°C fan) / 400F / gas 6.
- Toss the chicken cubes in the oil and spices.
- Thread onto skewers.
- Cook in the oven on a baking sheet for 8–10 minutes or until the chicken is cooked through and juicy.
- Meanwhile place the peaches in a pan with 6 tbsp water and the sugar. Simmer gently for 10–15 minutes until tender.
- Leave the peaches to cool, then remove the skins. Reserve the syrup.
- Tip the peaches, cooking syrup, extra virgin olive oil and chilli into a blender and blitz until smooth.
- Serve with the hot chicken.

Chicken Brochettes with Plum Chutney

54

- Use plums in place of the peaches and add a star anise whilst simmering.

55

SERVES 4

Chicken and Vegetable Brochettes

PREPARATION TIME 30 MINUTES

COOKING TIME 10 MINUTES

INGREDIENTS

4 chicken breasts, skinned and cut into chunks
1 tsp dried oregano
4 tbsp olive oil
½ lemon, juiced
salt and pepper
1 green pepper, deseeded and roughly chopped
1 red pepper, deseeded and roughly chopped
1 red onion, peeled and roughly chopped
8–10 cherry tomatoes, halved

- Toss the chicken chunks with oregano, oil, a little lemon juice and seasoning. Leave to marinate for 20 minutes.
- Thread the chicken onto soaked wooden skewers alternating with the peppers, onion and tomatoes.
- Grill or griddle until the chicken is golden and just cooked through, about 8–10 minutes.
- Serve with more lemon juice squeezed over and a little more salt.

Marinated Chicken Brochettes

56

- Use ready-made curry paste to marinate the chicken before cooking.

SERVES 4 57

Chicken Kebabs with Tabbouleh

- Marinate the chicken in oil, thyme, lemon juice and some seasoning for about 30 minutes.
- Meanwhile soak the bulghur wheat in the hot stock for 25–30 minutes until tender. Drain off any excess liquid and season. Stir through the parsley and juice of ½ lemon with the purslane and diced tomatoes.
- Thread the chicken onto skewers and barbecue or griddle for 8–10 minutes until golden and cooked through.
- Serve the chicken drizzled with a little lemon juice and the tabbouleh alongside.

PREPARATION TIME 40 MINUTES

COOKING TIME 10 MINUTES

INGREDIENTS

4 chicken breasts, skinned and cubed
2 tbsp olive oil
1 tbsp thyme leaves
1 tbsp lemon juice
salt and pepper
300 g / 10 oz / 1 ¼ cups bulghur wheat
400 ml / 14 fl. oz / 1 ½ cups chicken stock
1 bunch parsley, chopped
½ lemon, juiced
100 g / 3 ½ oz / ½ cup purslane lettuce
2 tomatoes, cored and diced

Chicken Kebabs with Garlic Sauce   58

- Stir 1 clove of crushed garlic and 4 tbsp extra virgin olive oil through 150 ml / 5 fl. oz / ½ cup plain yoghurt and drizzle over the chicken.

SERVES 4 59

Crispy Chicken Nuggets

- Cube the chicken and place in a bowl with the buttermilk. Refrigerate for at least 2 hours or even overnight.
- The next day, dip the cubes one at a time into the flour, egg then cornflakes and lay on a rack to dry slightly.
- Heat 1cm depth oil in a pan and fry the chicken in batches until golden on both sides and cooked through.
- Serve with ketchup for dipping

PREPARATION TIME 5 MINUTES
+ MARINATING TIME

COOKING TIME 10 MINUTES

INGREDIENTS

4 chicken breasts, skinned
300 ml / 10 fl. oz / 1 ¼ cups buttermilk
100 g / 3 ½ oz / ½ cup plain (all purpose) flour
2 eggs, beaten
200 g / 7 oz / ¾ cup cornflakes, lightly crushed
vegetable oil

Herby Chicken Nuggets   60

- Sprinkle mixed herbs over the cornflakes for a herby flavour.

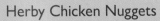

61

SERVES 2

Warm Thai Chicken Salad

Thai Chicken Salad with Lemongrass

62

- Make the dressing with 2 tbsp fish sauce, 1 tbsp sesame oil and a finely chopped lemongrass stalk instead of using soy and tamarind paste.

Chicken Salad with Coconut Dressing

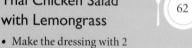
63

- Add 2–3 tbsp coconut milk for a rich creamy dressing.

PREPARATION TIME 15 MINUTES

COOKING TIME 15 MINUTES

INGREDIENTS

2 chicken breasts
2 tbsp olive oil
salt and pepper
250 g / 9 oz / 1 cup mixed salad leaves
10 cherry tomatoes, halved
1 red pepper, deseeded and finely sliced
100 g / 3 ½ oz / ½ cup beansprouts
1 orange, segmented
2 tbsp peanuts or cashew nuts, roughly chopped

FOR THE DRESSING

4 tbsp soy sauce
1 lime, juiced and zested
1 red chilli (chili), finely chopped
1 tsp tamarind paste
2 tsp soft brown sugar

- Heat the oil in a deep-sided frying pan and fry the chicken skin-side down until golden. Turn over and cook for a further 5–6 minutes until cooked through. Set aside, season and keep warm.
- Toss the cold salad ingredients together on a platter.
- Whisk together the ingredients for the dressing, then add to the frying pan and use a wooden spoon to deglaze, scraping any sticky bits into the sauce.
- Shred or slice the chicken and sit on top of the salad. Serve the dressing alongside to spoon over.

64

SERVES 4

Chicken and Tomato Coconut Soup

- Heat the oil in a wok or large pan and fry the onions until deep gold and sweet.
- Add the pepper, garlic, lemongrass, lime leaves and chillies and cook out for 2 minutes.
- Add the cubed chicken and allow to colour on all sides.
- Stir in the tamarind and fish sauce and sugar, then pour over the coconut milk and chicken stock.
- Lower the heat and leave to simmer for 15–20 minutes until the chicken is cooked through. Add the tomatoes and simmer for 5 minutes until just collapsing.
- Adjust the seasoning and stir in the lime juice just before serving.

Creamy Chicken Soup

 65

- Use all stock instead of coconut milk, then stir in 200 ml / 7 fl. oz / ¾ cup double (heavy) cream at the end of cooking.

PREPARATION TIME 15 MINUTES

COOKING TIME 40 MINUTES

INGREDIENTS

3 tbsp vegetable oil
½ bunch spring onions (scallions), finely sliced
1 red pepper, deseeded and chopped
2 cloves of garlic, finely chopped
2 stalks lemongrass, bruised
2 kaffir lime leaves
1 green chilli (chili), finely chopped
1 red chilli (chili), finely chopped
3–4 chicken breasts, skinned and cubed
2 tsp tamarind paste
2 tbsp fish sauce
1 tbsp soft brown sugar
400 ml / 14 fl. oz / 1 ½ cups coconut milk
300 ml / 10 fl. oz / 1 ¼ cups chicken stock
12 cherry tomatoes, halved
salt and pepper
1–2 limes, juiced

66

SERVES 4

Caramelised Chicken with Date Tabbouleh

- Soak the bulghur wheat in the hot stock for 10 minutes until tender. Drain off any excess liquid and season. Stir through the parsley, dates and juice of ½ lemon.
- Heat the oil in a pan and sauté the chicken until cooked through. Add the sugar, vinegar (carefully as it will splutter) and a little seasoning and stir to coat. Bubble up and thicken until sticky.
- Spoon the cous cous into serving glasses or ramekins, then serve with with the sticky chicken. Squeeze over a little lemon juice.

Apricot Tabbouleh

 67

- Try adding fresh, quartered, ripe apricots in summer for a fresh tasting tabbouleh.

PREPARATION TIME 20 MINUTES

COOKING TIME 10 MINUTES

INGREDIENTS

300 g / 10 oz / 1 ¼ cups bulghur wheat
400 ml / 14 fl. oz / 1 ½ cups chicken stock
1 bunch parsley, chopped
150 g / 5 oz / ⅔ cup dates, chopped
2 tbsp olive oil
4 chicken thighs, skinned, deboned and chopped
2 tbsp dark brown sugar
2 tbsp red wine vinegar
salt and pepper
1 lemon, juiced

68

MAKES 12

Chicken and Mimolette Fondants

PREPARATION TIME 20 MINUTES

COOKING TIME 20 MINUTES

INGREDIENTS

2 chicken breasts, skinned and finely diced
2 sprigs tarragon, chopped
100 g / 3 ½ oz / ½ cup Mimolette cheese, grated
100 ml / 3 ½ fl. oz / ½ cup double (heavy) cream
salt and pepper
500 g / 1 lb / 2 cups self-raising flour
80 g / 3 oz / ⅓ cup butter, melted
1 egg, beaten
250 ml / 9 fl. oz / 1 cup milk
30 g / 1 oz butter

- Preheat the oven to 200°C (180°C fan) / 400F / gas 6.
- Heat the 30 g butter in a pan and fry the chicken until golden and cooked. Add the tarragon, cheese, cream and seasoning and stir until the cheese has melted and the mixture is hot. Set aside.
- Tip the flour into a bowl and make a well in the centre. Whisk together the melted butter, egg and milk and pour into the flour. Mix together roughly until just about incorporated.
- Spoon into a lined muffin tin, filling each hole half full, then top with a generous spoonful of chicken mixture, then another spoonful of the batter to encase it. Bake for about 20 minutes until golden and cooked through at the centre.
- Leave to cool slightly before serving.

Chicken, Cheese and Sun-dried Tomato Fondants

69

- Add chopped sun-dried tomatoes to the mixture for a savoury punch.

70

SERVES 4

Kentucky Corn Chicken

PREPARATION TIME 20 MINUTES
+ MARINATING TIME

COOKING TIME 10 MINUTES

INGREDIENTS

12 chicken wings
300 ml / 10 fl. oz / 1 ¼ cups buttermilk
100 g / 3 ½ oz / ½ cup plain (all purpose) flour
2 eggs, beaten
200 g / 7 oz / ¾ cup cornflakes, lightly crushed

few drops hot sauce
vegetable oil

- Place the chicken wings in a bowl with the buttermilk. Refrigerate for at least 2 hours or even overnight.
- The next day, add some hot sauce to the eggs, then dip the chicken wings one at a time into the flour, eggs, then cornflakes. Lay them on a rack to dry slightly.
- Fill a pan ⅔ full with vegetable oil and heat to 180°C / 350F and fry the chicken wings in batches until golden on both sides and cooked through.
- Serve immediately.

Kentucky Polenta Chicken

71

- Substitute the cornflakes for coarse polenta for a crispy result.

72

MAKES 12

Chicken and Cheese Muffins

Chicken, Cheese and Spinach Muffins

73

- Add 100 g / 3 ½ oz / ½ cup wilted finely chopped spinach to the mix.

Chicken Tomato Cheese Muffins

74

- Use chopped sun-dried tomatoes for a richer flavour.

PREPARATION TIME 15 MINUTES

COOKING TIME 20–25 MINUTES

INGREDIENTS

225 g / 8 oz / 1 cup self-raising flour
50 g / 1 ¾ oz / ¼ cup rye flour
1 tsp baking powder
½ tsp bicarbonate of (baking) soda
1 tsp salt
1 tsp English mustard powder
pinch cayenne
125 g / 4 oz / ½ cup strong Cheddar, grated
120 g / 4 oz / ½ cup cooked chicken, finely chopped
6 tbsp vegetable oil
150 g / 5 oz / ⅔ cup plain or Greek yoghurt
125 ml / 4 fl. oz / ½ cup milk
1 egg

- Preheat the oven to 200°C (180°C fan) / 400F / gas 6. Line a 12-hole muffin tin with paper cases.
- Mix together all the dry ingredients in a large bowl, adding the cheese and chicken.
- In another bowl, mix together the liquid ingredients with a fork.
- Pour the liquid ingredients into the dry, mixing with a fork, but don't over-mix – the muffins will be lighter with a lumpy batter.
- Spoon into the cases and bake for 20–25 minutes until golden and risen.
- Allow to cool on a rack before eating.

SERVES 4

Chicken and Mushroom Croustade

75

PREPARATION TIME 10 MINUTES

COOKING TIME 15 MINUTES

INGREDIENTS

40 g / 1 oz butter
1 tbsp olive oil
1 shallot, finely chopped
1 clove of garlic, crushed
2 chicken thighs, skinned and deboned, cut into chunks
150 g / 5 oz / ⅔ cup chestnut mushrooms, quartered
100 ml / 3 ½ fl. oz / ½ cup white wine
150 ml / 5 fl. oz / ⅔ cup double (heavy) cream
salt and pepper
½ bunch parsley, finely chopped
½ lemon, juiced
4 thick slices sourdough bread

- Heat the butter and oil in a pan and sweat the shallot and garlic until softened.
- Add the chicken and cook briskly for a few minutes, then add the mushrooms and cook until they start to soften.
- Add the white wine and reduce until syrupy, then add the cream and seasoning and simmer until thickened.
- Stir through the parsley.
- Toast the bread. Squeeze a little lemon juice into the chicken mixture and adjust the seasoning, then spoon over the toast and serve.

Chicken and Bacon Croustade

76

- Add 2 rashers of diced and cooked streaky bacon to the chicken.

77

SERVES 4

Chicken with Orange and Sesame Seeds

PREPARATION TIME 5 MINUTES

COOKING TIME 10 MINUTES

INGREDIENTS

2 tbsp vegetable oil
1 shallot, finely chopped
2 chicken breasts, skinned and chopped
2 oranges, zested and juiced
200 ml / 7 fl. oz / ¾ cup chicken stock
1 tbsp soy sauce
2 tbsp sesame seeds
salt and pepper

- Heat the oil in a wok and fry the shallot and chicken briskly until golden.
- Add the orange zest, juice and chicken stock and simmer for 5 minutes until reduced, then stir in the soy.
- Sprinkle over the sesame seeds, season and serve with white rice.

Citrus Chicken with Sesame Seeds

78

- Try adding lime or grapefruit juice with the orange for zing.

SERVES 4

Curried Chicken Sandwich

79

- Cube the chicken, toss with the curry paste and leave to marinate in the refrigerator for 30 minutes.
- Griddle or fry the chicken in a pan until golden and sizzling and just cooked through. Squeeze over the lemon juice, season and set aside.
- Meanwhile whisk the yoghurt with the seasoning and mint.
- Slice the rolls in half and spread some yoghurt dressing on the bottom halves. Spoon the chicken on top and add tomatoes and onion. Serve.

PREPARATION TIME 10 MINUTES

COOKING TIME 10 MINUTES

INGREDIENTS

4 chicken breasts, skinned
4 tbsp tikka masala paste
100 ml / 3 ½ fl.oz / ½ cup plain yoghurt
salt and pepper
½ lemon, juiced
½ bunch mint, finely chopped
2 tomatoes, thickly sliced
1 red onion, peeled and finely sliced
4 bread rolls

Spicy Curry Chicken Sandwich

80

- Adding a chopped red chilli (chili) to the marinade will add fire to the chicken.

SERVES 4

Chicken and Vegetable Salad

81

- You could leave the cauliflower florets raw, or simply steam for a couple of minutes over simmering water.
- Shred the chicken and tip into a bowl with the sweetcorn. beans, pepper and cauliflower florets.
- Whisk together the oil, lime and seasoning and toss with the salad.

PREPARATION TIME 10 MINUTES

COOKING TIME 5 MINUTES

INGREDIENTS

2 chicken breasts, cooked
½ head cauliflower, separated into florets
250 g / 9 oz / 1 cup sweetcorn
150 g / 5 oz / ⅔ cup green beans, diced
1 red pepper, deseeded and finely chopped
2 tbsp extra virgin olive oil
1 lime, juiced
salt and pepper

Chicken and Bean Salad

82

- Add 400 g / 14 oz / 1 ½ cups canned cannellini beans, drained for bulk.

83

MAKES 12

Cheesy Chicken Muffins

PREPARATION TIME 20 MINUTES

COOKING TIME 20 MINUTES

....

INGREDIENTS

2 chicken breasts, skinned
and finely diced
1 tsp dried thyme
100 g / 3 ½ oz / ½ cup red Leicester
cheese, cubed
100 ml / 3 ½ fl. oz / ½ cup crème
fraiche
salt and pepper
500 g / 1 lb / 2 cups self-raising flour
80 g / 3 oz / ⅓ cup butter, melted
1 egg, beaten
250 ml / 9 fl. oz / 1 cup milk
30 g / 1 oz butter

- Preheat the oven to 200°C (180°C fan) / 400F / gas 6.
- Heat the butter in a pan and fry the chicken until golden and cooked. Add the thyme, cheese, crème fraiche and seasoning and stir until the cheese has melted and the mixture is hot. Set aside.
- Tip the flour into a bowl and make a well in the centre. Whisk together the wet ingredients and pour into the flour. Mix together roughly until just about incorporated.
- Spoon into a lined muffin tin, filling each hole half full, then top with a generous spoonful of chicken mixture, then another spoonful of the batter to encase it. Bake for about 20 minutes until golden and cooked through at the centre.
- Leave to cool slightly before serving.

Italian Chicken Fondants   84

- Use mixed Italian herbs instead of thyme and diced Gorgonzola instead of red Leicester.

85

SERVES 4

Crunchy Chicken Wings with Asparagus

PREPARATION TIME 20 MINUTES
+ MARINATING TIME

COOKING TIME 15 MINUTES

....

INGREDIENTS

8 chicken wings
300 ml / 10 fl. oz / 1 ¼ cups
buttermilk
100 g / 3 ½ oz / ½ cup plain
(all purpose) flour
2 eggs, beaten
200 g / 7 oz / ¾ cup breadcrumbs,
vegetable oil
16 asparagus stalks, trimmed
40 g / 1 oz butter
salt and pepper
chopped fresh thyme, to garnish

- Place the chicken in a bowl with the buttermilk. Refrigerate for at least 2 hours or even overnight.
- Dip the chicken wings one at a time into the flour, egg then breadcrumbs and lay on a rack to dry slightly.
- Heat enough oil in a pan to be two-thirds full. It is hot enough when a cube of bread dropped in sizzles immediately. Fry the chicken in batches until golden on both sides and cooked through. Drain on kitchen paper.
- Steam the asparagus for 4–5 minutes until just tender, then toss in butter and seasoning. Serve with the chicken, scattered with fresh thyme.

Kicking Chicken Wings   86

- Spice up the breadcrumbs with cayenne, mustard and paprika.

87

SERVES 4

Tequila Chicken Kebabs

Bloody Mary Chicken

88

- Try using tomato juice, vodka and parsley in the marinade and cook the same way.

Festival Tequila Chicken

89

- Add chopped red and green peppers to the skewers, between each chunk of chicken.

PREPARATION TIME 5 MINUTES
+ MARINATING TIME

COOKING TIME 10 MINUTES

....

INGREDIENTS

4 chicken breasts, skinned and cubed
150 ml / 5 fl. oz / ⅔ cup tequila
zest of 1 lime
1 red chilli (chili), sliced
salt and pepper
2 limes, sliced
½ bunch fresh coriander (cilantro), chopped

- Marinate the chicken in tequila, lime zest, chilli and seasoning for 30 minutes.
- Thread onto metal or soaked wooden skewers, alternating with slices of lime.
- Griddle over high heat until golden and cooked through.
- Reduce the marinade in a small pan until syrupy.
- Sprinkle with coriander and serve with the reduced sauce drizzled over.

90

SERVES 4

Chicken Tandoori with Bulghur

PREPARATION TIME 25 MINUTES
+ MARINATING TIME

COOKING TIME 10 MINUTES

....

INGREDIENTS

4 skinless chicken breasts,
cut into long strips
300 g / 10 oz / 1 ¼ cups bulghur
wheat
400 ml / 14 fl. oz / 1 ½ cups chicken
stock
salt and pepper

FOR THE MARINADE

300 ml / 10 fl. oz /1 ¼ cups plain
yoghurt
1 tsp ground cumin
1 tsp ground coriander (cilantro)
1 tsp garam masala
1 tsp ground cinnamon
1 ½ tsp tandoori chilli (chili) powder
1 tsp caster (superfine) sugar
1 clove garlic, minced
salt and pepper

- Prepare the tandoori marinade by mixing together
  all the ingredients for the marinade in a mixing bowl.
  Add the chicken, mix well, then cover and chill for at
  least 1 hour.
- Meanwhile soak the bulghur wheat in the hot stock for
  25–30 minutes until tender. Drain off any excess liquid
  and season.
- Pre-heat the grill to hot. Remove the chicken from
  the marinade, shaking off any excess, and thread onto
  soaked wooden skewers.
- Grill for 8–10 minutes, turning occasionally until
  lightly charred and cooked through.
- Place the tandoori chicken skewers on top of the
  bulghur and serve.

Chicken Tandoori with Tzatziki 91

- Toss ½ grated cucumber with 4 tbsp plain
  yoghurt and ¼ bunch chopped mint leaves
  and a little seasoning and serve spooned
  over the chicken.

92

SERVES 4

Chicken and Fig Kebabs

PREPARATION TIME 15 MINUTES

COOKING TIME 10 MINUTES

....

INGREDIENTS

4 chicken breasts, skinned and cut
into chunks
8 ripe figs, halved
2 tbsp olive oil
salt and pepper
250 g / 9 oz / 1 cup cous cous
250 ml / 9 fl. oz / 1 cup chicken or
vegetable stock
½ lemon, juiced
1 bunch chervil, roughly chopped
2 tbsp pine nuts, toasted

- Thread the chicken pieces onto metal or wooden
  skewers, alternating with the halved figs and brush
  with oil. Season.
- Place the cous cous in a bowl, cover with the hot stock
  and clingfilm the bowl. Leave for 10 minutes or so until
  tender, then fork through the grains and add the lemon,
  herbs and pine nuts.
- Griddle the chicken kebabs over high heat for about
  8–10 minutes until the chicken is golden and cooked
  through.
- Serve the kebabs with the cous cous alongside.

Sticky Chicken Kebabs 93

- Brush the chicken and figs with a
  little runny honey during cooking.

94

MAKES 40

Balsamic Chicken and Tomato Crostini

- Preheat the oven to 200°C (180°C fan) / 400F / gas 6.
- Cut the baguette into slices about ½ cm thick. You should get around 40 out of a baguette. Place on baking sheets and brush lightly with olive oil. Bake in the oven for about 5–10 minutes until pale gold. Remove and leave to cool.
- Heat 2–3 tbsp olive oil in a pan and sauté the chicken and garlic until golden. Deglaze with balsamic and thyme leaves and season. Toss in the sesame seeds until coated.
- Toss the chicken with the cherry tomatoes and spoon onto the crostini and serve.

PREPARATION TIME 20 MINUTES

COOKING TIME 10 MINUTES

INGREDIENTS

1 baguette
olive oil
400 g / 14 oz / 1 ½ cups diced chicken meat, preferably from the thighs
1 large clove of garlic, crushed
2–3 tbsp balsamic vinegar
2 tbsp thyme leaves
2 tbsp sesame seeds
salt and pepper
200 g / 7 oz / ¾ cup cherry tomatoes, quartered

Persian Chicken Crostini

95

- Twist the recipe by using pomegranate molasses instead of balsamic for a sweet-sour flavour.

96

SERVES 8

Savoury Chicken Carrot Cake

- Preheat oven to 190°C (170°C fan) / 375F / gas 5.
- Whisk the eggs and sugar together until pale and thick.
- Sieve the flours, baking powder and salt into a bowl, then fold into the eggs. Stir in the ricotta and oil until incorporated.
- Fold in the chicken and carrots with the thyme until well combined.
- Grease and line a loaf tin, then pour the mixture in.
- Bake in the oven for about 40 minutes until a skewer inserted into the middle comes out clean.
- Remove to a wire rack and allow to cool before slicing.

PREPARATION TIME 25 MINUTES

COOKING TIME 40 MINUTES

INGREDIENTS

3 eggs
1 tsp sugar
235 g / 8 oz / 1 cup plain (all purpose) flour
60 g / 2 oz / ¼ cup potato flour
2 tsp baking powder
½ tsp salt
6 tbsp olive oil
2 tbsp ricotta
200 g / 6 ½ oz / ¾ cup cooked chicken, finely chopped
2 large carrots, peeled and grated
3 sprigs thyme leaves, chopped

Crunchy Chicken Carrot Cake

97

- 2–3 tbsp finely chopped walnuts stirred into the mix will add crunch.

98

SERVES 4

Chicken, Ham and Apple Bagels

PREPARATION TIME 10 MINUTES

COOKING TIME 5 MINUTES

INGREDIENTS

4 sesame bagels
4 slices Parma ham
2 chicken breasts, cooked and sliced
1 red apple, cut into matchsticks and
tossed with a little lemon juice
2 tbsp grain or Dijon mustard
salt and pepper

- Split the bagels and toast lightly.
- Heat a dry frying pan and fry the Parma ham slices until crisp and darkened on both sides – about 2 minutes per side.
- Spread the bottom bagel halves with a little mustard, then lay the ham slices on top. Place the chicken slices on top and then arrange the apple matchsticks. Season and sandwich with the remaining bagel halves.

Chicken and Blue Cheese Bagels   99
- Slices of Gorgonzola cheese would make a flavoursome addition.

100

SERVES 2

Chicken and Broccoli Salad

PREPARATION TIME 10 MINUTES

COOKING TIME 3 MINUTES

INGREDIENTS

2 chicken breasts, cooked
1 head broccoli, separated into
florets
1 red pepper, deseeded and sliced
2 ripe tomatoes, cored and cut into
wedges
200 ml / 7 fl. oz / ¾ cup crème
fraîche
1 clove of garlic, crushed
3 tbsp Parmesan, grated
1 tbsp lemon juice
1 tbsp chopped fresh chives
salt and pepper

- Shred the chicken into small pieces and place in a bowl.
- Steam the broccoli florets for 3 minutes until crisp-tender, then add to the chicken with the peppers and tomatoes.
- Mix together the crème fraîche, garlic, Parmesan, lemon, chives and seasoning.
- Toss the salad in the dressing and serve.

Light Chicken Salad   101
- Use yoghurt instead of crème fraîche and forego the Parmesan.

102
SERVES 6–8

Chicken Pâté in a Pastry Crust

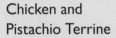

Chicken and Bacon Terrine

103

- Add 220 g / 8 oz / ¾ cup chopped streaky bacon for extra flavour or try using rabbit meat.

Chicken and Pistachio Terrine

 104

- Add 150 g / 5 oz / 1 ½ cups shelled pistachios to the mix before cooking.

PREPARATION TIME 30 MINUTES + MARINATING TIME

COOKING TIME 40 MINUTES

INGREDIENTS

500 g / 1 lb / 2 cups skinless chicken
3 tbsp olive oil
200 ml / 7 fl. oz / ¾ cup white wine
1 tsp coriander (cilantro) seeds, crushed
1 tbsp thyme leaves
2 tbsp chervil, chopped
2 tbsp parsley, chopped
2 eggs
2 tbsp double (heavy) cream
salt and pepper
500 g / 1 lb shortcrust pastry
flour, for dusting
1 egg, beaten

- Cut the chicken into large chunks and marinate with the wine and oil for 1 hour.
- Preheat the oven to 200°C (180°C fan) / 400F / gas 6.
- Remove the meat from the marinade and place half in a food processor, add the herbs and spices, eggs and cream and seasoning and pulse until finely chopped. Stir in the remaining chicken pieces.
- Roll out two thirds of the pastry on a floured surface and use to line the base and sides of a small loaf tin. Spoon in the chicken mixture. Roll out the remaining pastry to make a lid. Wet the pastry edges with water and place the lid on top, pressing the edges to seal. Cut a steam hole in the top and brush with beaten egg. Bake for 20 minutes.
- Reduce the heat to 180°C (160°C fan) / 350F / gas 4 and cook for a further 20 minutes until deep golden brown.
- Leave to rest for at least 30 minutes before slicing.

105

SERVES 4

Chicken, Apple and Peanut Skewers

Chicken and Pear Skewers

106

- This works well with slightly under-ripe pears cut into chunks.

Chicken Goats' Cheese Skewers

107

- Add chunks of goats' cheese to the skewers.

PREPARATION TIME 15 MINUTES

COOKING TIME 25 MINUTES

INGREDIENTS

250 g / 9 oz / 1 cup Bramley apples
250 g / 9 oz / 1 cup Cox apples
1 tbsp sugar (optional, depending on tartness of apples and usage)
2 cloves
2 tbsp water
1 tbsp cider vinegar
2 chicken breasts, skinned and cut into bite-size pieces
1 eating apple, cored and cut into wedges
30 g / 1 oz butter, melted
2 tbsp peanuts, crushed

- Peel and core the Bramley and Cox apples and cut into chunks. Place in a pan with the sugar, cloves, vinegar and water and cover with a lid.

- Cook over a low heat for 10–15 minutes, checking occasionally, until the apples are very soft and fluffy. Beat to a puree and remove the cloves.

- Thread the chicken onto skewers with the eating apple and brush with melted butter whilst cooking over a medium griddle. Cook until golden and the apple softens.

- Sprinkle with peanuts and serve with the apple sauce to dip.

108

SERVES 4

Sesame Chicken with Mango Chutney

- Roll the chicken pieces in oil, then in breadcrumbs mixed with sesame, 5 spice and seasoning.
- Thread the chicken onto soaked wooden skewers and thread the mango and spring onions onto smaller skewers or cocktail sticks. Griddle the chicken over a medium heat until cooked through – about 8 minutes. Griddle the mango sticks for 1–2 minutes to heat through.
- Serve with the mango chutney.

PREPARATION TIME 15 MINUTES

COOKING TIME 8–10 MINUTES

INGREDIENTS

4 chicken thighs, skinned, deboned and cut into chunks
2 tbsp olive oil
150 g / 5 oz / ½ cup dried breadcrumbs
2 tbsp sesame seeds
1 tsp Chinese 5 spice powder
salt and pepper
100 g / 3 ½ oz / ½ cup mango chutney
½ mango, peeled and cut into small cubes
2–3 spring onions (scalions), sliced

Indian Sesame Skewers

109

- Substitute the 5 spice for garam masala and serve with hot lime pickle.

110

SERVES 2

Grilled Pepper Chicken

- Coat the chicken with oil, then press peppercorns and sesame seeds onto both sides and season with salt.
- Heat a griddle pan and cook for 5 minutes on each side until cooked through. Leave to rest.
- Mix the yoghurt with the cucumber and seasoning.
- Serve the chicken sliced , yoghurt dressing spooned alongside with some salad.

PREPARATION TIME 10 MINUTES

COOKING TIME 10–12 MINUTES

INGREDIENTS

2 chicken breasts, skinned
2 tbsp olive oil
1 tbsp mixed peppercorns, crushed
1 tbsp white and black sesame seeds
salt
200 ml / 7 fl. oz / ¾ cup plain yoghurt
½ cucumber, cut into fine batons
mixed salad leaves

Grilled Chicken with Hot Peppercorn Sauce

111

- Stir the crushed peppercorns into 200 ml / 7 fl. oz / ¾ cup double (heavy) cream and simmer until thickened.

112

SERVES 4

Chicken Tandoori and Mint Brochettes

PREPARATION TIME 25 MINUTES
+ MARINATING TIME

COOKING TIME 10 MINUTES

INGREDIENTS

4 chicken thighs, skinned, deboned
and cubed
1 cucumber, thickly sliced
1 tsp salt
150 ml / 5 fl. oz / ⅔ cup plain
yoghurt
½ bunch mint leaves, finely sliced
1 clove of garlic, crushed

FOR THE MARINADE
1 tsp ground cumin
1 tsp ground coriander (cilantro)
1 tsp garam masala
1 tsp ground cinnamon
1 ½ tsp tandoori chilli (chili) powder
1 tsp caster (superfine) sugar
1 clove garlic, minced
salt and pepper

- Prepare the tandoori marinade by mixing together all the ingredients for the marinade in a mixing bowl. Add the chicken, mix well, then cover and chill for at least 1 hour.
- Meanwhile toss the cucumber with the salt and leave to drain in a sieve to draw out excess water.
- Mix the yoghurt with the mint, garlic and seasoning and set aside.
- Thread the chicken onto skewers and griddle or barbecue for about 10 minutes until cooked through.
- Pat the cucumber dry, then serve alongside the skewers and minted yoghurt.

Chicken Tandoori Pittas
113

- Stuff the chicken pieces and cucumber into split pittas and drizzle with the yoghurt.

114

SERVES 4

Spicy Chicken Coconut Soup

PREPARATION TIME 15 MINUTES

COOKING TIME 25–30 MINUTES

INGREDIENTS

3 tbsp vegetable oil
1 onion, peeled and finely sliced
1 yellow pepper, deseeded and
chopped
2 cloves of garlic, finely chopped
2 stalks lemongrass, bruised
2 kaffir lime leaves
1 green chilli (chili), finely chopped
1 red chilli (chili), finely chopped
3–4 chicken breasts, skinned
and cubed
2 tsp tamarind paste
2 tbsp fish sauce
1 tbsp soft brown sugar or palm
sugar
400 ml / 14 fl. oz / 1 ½ cups coconut
milk
300 ml / 10 fl. oz / 1 ¼ cups chicken
stock
salt and pepper
1–2 limes, juiced

- Heat the oil in a wok or large pan and fry the onion until deep gold and sweet.
- Add the pepper, garlic and spices and cook out for 2 minutes.
- Add the cubed chicken and allow to colour on all sides.
- Stir in the tamarind and fish sauce and sugar, then pour over the coconut milk and chicken stock.
- Lower the heat and leave to simmer for 15–20 minutes until the chicken is cooked through.
- Adjust the seasoning and stir in the lime juice just before serving.

Quick Coconut Soup
115

- Stir in 2–3 tbsp Thai curry paste instead of the spices, tamarind and fish sauce for very fast supper.

SERVES 4

Honey and Mustard Chicken with Polenta

116

Honey Mustard Chicken with Croutons

 117

- For a speedy version of this dish, roast cubed bread croutons around the chicken and toss with the salad.

Honey Mustard Chicken with Noodles

118

- Toss with cooked egg noodles or pasta for a hearty meal.

PREPARATION TIME 20 MINUTES

COOKING TIME
1 HOUR 10 MINUTES

INGREDIENTS

225 g / 9 oz / 1 cup polenta
2 tbsp olive oil
4 tbsp runny honey
2 tbsp grain mustard
salt and pepper
4 drumsticks, skin on
2 tbsp sesame seeds
100 ml / 3 ½ fl. oz / ½ cup olive oil
16 cherry tomatoes, halved
200 g / 7 oz / ¾ cup rocket (arugula)
½ lemon, juiced

- Whisk the polenta slowly into a large pan filled with 1.7 L / 3 pints / 6 cups salted boiling water. As soon as it begins to boil it will start to 'blip', so cover with a lid slightly askew and turn the heat down to minimum.

- When it begins to thicken, stir every 5 minutes or so very thoroughly, ensuring you push the spoon down into the sides of the pan. Cook for about 45 minutes until it begins to have the consistency of mashed potato. Season generously.

- Oil a tray and tip the polenta out onto to it. Spread the polenta to about 2.5 cm thick. Leave the polenta to cool for about 30 minutes and then cut out equally-sized cubes. Preheat the oven to 200°C (180°C fan) / 400F / gas 6.

- Meanwhile, mix together the honey, mustard, 2 tbsp of oil and seasoning and coat the chicken. Roast in a foil-lined roasting tin for about 25 minutes until golden and sticky. Toss in the sesame seeds.

- Heat 100 ml oil in a deep-sided pan and shallow-fry the polenta cubes on all sides until golden, turning them frequently. Remove to kitchen paper to drain and season.

- Toss the polenta cubes in a bowl with the tomatoes and rocket and drizzle with a little lemon juice. Serve with the chicken.

119
SERVES 2

Crispy Chicken with Cherry Soup

PREPARATION TIME 30 MINUTES

COOKING TIME 15 MINUTES

INGREDIENTS

2 chicken breasts, skinned and thickly sliced
3 tbsp flour, seasoned
1 egg, beaten
75 g / 2 ½ oz / ⅓ cup breadcrumbs
1 tsp dried thyme
salt and pepper
2 tbsp vegetable oil
½ cucumber, halved and deseeded
1 green apple, halved and cored
ground ginger or cumin to garnish
200 g / 7 oz / ¾ cup cherries, stoned
200 ml / 7 fl. oz / ¾ cup light red or rose wine
1–2 tbsp caster (superfine) sugar

- Lay the flour, egg and breadcrumbs out on separate plates. Stir the thyme into the breadcrumbs. Using one hand (to keep the other clean), dip each chicken strip alternately into the flour, egg and breadcrumbs and thoroughly coat.
- Once all have been coated, heat the oil in a pan and fry on all sides until golden and the chicken is cooked through – about 6–8 minutes. Drain on kitchen paper and keep warm in a low oven.
- To make the salad, slice the cucumber into thin half moons. Do the same with the apple halves and mix with the cucumber. Chill until needed.
- To make the soup, simply bring the cherries to a simmer in the wine and add 1 tbsp sugar. Leave to simmer gently for 5 minutes or until the cherries start to soften. Taste – you may want more sugar, in which case continue cooking for a few minutes to dissolve the sugar. Chill until needed.
- Serve the warm chicken with the salad, sprinkled with ground ginger or cumin and chilled soup.

120
SERVES 4

Tandoori Chicken Salad

PREPARATION TIME 15 MINUTES

COOKING TIME 15 MINUTES

INGREDIENTS

4 chicken breasts, skinned
2 tbsp vegetable oil
salt and pepper
1 red pepper, deseeded and finely diced
1 yellow pepper, deseeded and finely diced
225 g / 8 oz / 1 cup mixed salad leaves
200 ml / 7 fl. oz / ¾ cup plain yoghurt
½ tsp ground cinnamon
1 tsp paprika
1–2 tsp garam masala
pinch cayenne pepper
12 mint leaves, finely shredded

- Pan fry the chicken in the oil with seasoning until cooked through and golden on both sides – about 12–15 minutes. Set aside to rest.
- Toss the salad leaves with the diced peppers.
- Mix the yoghurt with the spices and mint, season.
- Slice the chicken thickly, serve on top of the salad, drizzled with the tandoori dressing.

121

SERVES 4

Chicken, Chickpea and Asparagus Salad

- Steam the asparagus over simmering water for 3–4 minutes until the stems are tender to the point of a knife.
- Slice the chicken and set aside. Gently toss together the chickpeas and onion slices.
- Whisk together the mustard and lemon juice, then whisk in the oil, seasoning and parsley and drizzle over the chickpea salad.
- Serve the salad topped with chicken slices, with the asparagus stems draped over. Finish with the rocket and any leftover dressing.

PREPARATION TIME 10 MINUTES

COOKING TIME 5 MINUTES

INGREDIENTS

4 chicken breasts, cooked
1 bunch asparagus, ends trimmed
400 g / 14 oz / 1 ½ cups canned chickpeas, drained
½ red onion, peeled and finely sliced
½ lemon, juiced
1 tbsp Dijon mustard
80 ml / 2 ½ fl. oz / ⅓ cup extra virgin olive oil
salt and pepper
¼ bunch parsley, finely chopped
handful of rcket (arugula) leaves

Chicken Vol au Vents

122

SERVES 6

PREPARATION TIME 20 MINUTES

COOKING TIME 30–35 MINUTES

INGREDIENTS

350 g / 12 oz / 1 ½ cups ready rolled puff pastry
1 egg, beaten, 1 tbsp breadcrumbs
3 tbsp butter
2 chicken thighs, skinned and deboned, meat chopped
300 g / 10 oz / 1 ½ cups mixed wild mushrooms, chopped
2 sprigs thyme leaves
2 tbsp plain (all purpose) flour
300 ml / 10 fl. oz / 1 ¼ cups milk
2 tbsp Parmesan, grated
salt and pepper

- Roll the pastry out on a floured surface to 2.5 cm / ¼ in thick. Cut out six 7 cm / 3 in circles or flower shapes with a pastry cutter, and score a smaller circle (or flower) just inside the rim.
- Place on a baking sheet and chill for 30 minutes. Preheat the oven to 200°C (180°C fan) / 400F / gas 6.
- Brush the pastry cases with a little egg, sprinkle with breadcrumbs and bake for 20 minutes or until risen and golden. Leave to cool, then carefully remove the lids and scoop out the centres.
- Melt the butter in a pan and cook the chicken and mushrooms with thyme and seasoning until any excess liquid has evaporated.
- Stir in the flour and cook out for 2 minutes, then whisk in the milk and simmer for 5–10 minutes until thickened and smooth. Whisk in the Parmesan.
- Spoon into the pastry cases, replace the lids and serve.

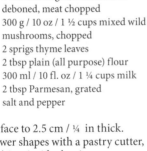

Oat-crusted Chicken Bites

123

SERVES 4

PREPARATION TIME 10 MINUTES

COOKING TIME 10 MINUTES

INGREDIENTS

4 chicken breasts, skinned
salt and pepper
3 tbsp flour
2 eggs, beaten
200 g / 6 ½ oz / ¾ cup coarse oatmeal
½ bunch parsley, finely chopped
olive oil

- Cut the chicken into bite-size pieces. Season, then dunk each chicken piece into flour, then egg then the oatmeal mixed with the parsley.
- Heat the oil in a large pan and fry in batches until golden and crisp and the chicken is cooked through – 8–10 minutes.
- Skewer with toothpicks and serve hot.

124

SERVES 4

Chicken Yakitori

Chicken and Aubergine Yakitori

125

- Add chunks of aubergine (eggplant) with the chicken to tenderise and soak up the sauces before cooking.

Sweet Chilli Chicken

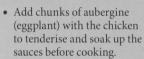
126

- Use sweet chilli sauce on half the skewers instead of teriyaki sauce.

PREPARATION TIME 10 MINUTES
+ MARINATING TIME
COOKING TIME 10 MINUTES

....

INGREDIENTS

4 chicken breasts, skinned
2 tbsp teriyaki sauce, plus extra to serve
2 tbsp soy sauce
1 tsp fresh ginger, grated
1 clove of garlic, crushed

- Cut the chicken into chunks.
- Mix together the remaining ingredients and coat the chicken thoroughly. Marinate for 30–60 minutes.
- Thread onto soaked wooden skewers and cook under a medium grill, basting with any remaining marinade until cooked and sticky.
- Serve hot with teriyaki sauce for dipping.

127

SERVES 4

Caramelised Chicken Drumsticks

- Preheat the oven to 200°C (180°C fan) / 400F / gas 6.
- Mix together the sauce ingredients and simmer in a pan for 5 minutes, then coat the drumsticks thoroughly in the sauce.
- Lay the drumsticks in a foil-lined roasting tin and roast in the oven for about 25 minutes until golden and cooked through. If they look like they are burning, cover with foil.
- Meanwhile arrange the peppers in a bowl and soak the rice noodles according to packet instructions.
- Serve the hot chicken with the cold crunchy peppers and noodles.

Caramelised Chicken Wraps

128

- Pull the meat from the cooked drumsticks and wrap in tortillas with the peppers and a little shredded lettuce.

PREPARATION TIME 10 MINUTES

COOKING TIME 30 MINUTES

INGREDIENTS

8 chicken drumsticks
olive oil
2 yellow peppers, deseeded and finely sliced
rice noodles, to serve

FOR THE SAUCE

4 tbsp white wine vinegar
3–4 tbsp soy sauce
2–3 tbsp tomato ketchup
1 tbsp soft brown sugar
1 tbsp runny honey
1 tbsp Dijon mustard
1 tsp fresh ginger, grated
1 tsp paprika
pinch dried chilli (chili) flakes
salt and pepper

129

SERVES 4

Bollywood Soup

- Heat the oil in a pan and sauté the onion for about 10 minutes or until golden-brown. Add the garlic, chilli and ginger and fry for another minute.
- Add the spices and stir well, then add the chicken and sweet potato to the sauce and pour in the coconut milk and stock. Cook at a simmer for around 20 minutes until the chicken and sweet potato are tender.
- Adjust the seasoning and sprinkle with coriander leaves before serving.

Jewelled Bollywood Soup

130

- For extra bling add diced vari-coloured peppers.

PREPARATION TIME 15 MINUTES

COOKING TIME 40 MINUTES

INGREDIENTS

3 tbsp vegetable oil
1 onion, peeled and finely sliced
2 cloves of garlic, chopped
1 red chilli (chili), deseeded and finely chopped
1 tsp fresh ginger, grated
1 tsp ground coriander (cilantro)
pinch turmeric
½ tsp ground cumin
½ tsp garam masala
1 tsp paprika
1 tsp mustard seeds
2 sweet potatoes, peeled and chopped
450 g / 1 lb / 2 cups chicken thigh meat, skinned and diced
400 ml / 14 fl. oz / 1 ½ cups canned coconut milk
300 ml / 10 fl. oz / 1 ¼ cups chicken stock
coriander (cilantro) leaves, to garnish

131

SERVES 4

Thai Chicken and Coconut Soup

PREPARATION TIME 15 MINUTES

COOKING TIME 25–30 MINUTES

INGREDIENTS

3 tbsp vegetable oil
1 onion, peeled and finely sliced
1 red pepper, deseeded and roughly chopped
1 red chilli (chili), finely sliced
2 stalks lemongrass, bruised
3–4 chicken breasts, skinned and cubed
2 tbsp red Thai curry paste
2 tbsp fish sauce
400 ml / 14 fl. oz / 1 ½ cups coconut milk
200 ml / 7 fl. oz / ¾ cup chicken stock
salt and pepper
1–2 limes, juiced
½ bunch coriander (cilantro), finely chopped, stalks reserved

- Heat the oil in a wok or large pan and fry the onion and pepper until deep gold and sweet.
- Add the curry paste and chilli and cook out for 2 minutes.
- Add the cubed chicken and lemongrass, and allow to colour on all sides.
- Stir in the fish sauce, then pour over the coconut milk and chicken stock and add the coriander stalks. Lower the heat and leave to simmer for 15–20 minutes until the chicken is cooked through.
- Adjust the seasoning and stir in the lime juice and chopped coriander just before serving in deep warmed bowls.

Thai Chicken Noodle Soup

132

- Add 1 nest dried egg noodles per person to cook in the liquid for a more substantial soup.

133

SERVES 4

Chicken and Rice Sesame Salad

PREPARATION TIME 20 MINUTES

COOKING TIME 15 MINUTES

INGREDIENTS

240 ml / 8 ½ oz / 1 cup rice
480 ml / 1 pint / 2 cups weak chicken or vegetable stock
2 chicken breasts, cooked and shredded
2 sticks celery, finely sliced
2 tbsp lime juice
4 tbsp olive oil
salt and pepper
1 tbsp sesame seeds
1 green chilli (chili), finely sliced

- Measure the rice (in volume) into a saucepan and cover with the stock. Cover with a lid and cook for 10 minutes.
- Remove from the heat and leave to sit for 5 minutes with the lid on. Then remove the lid and leave to cool a little in a bowl while you prepare the remaining salad ingredients.
- Toss the celery and chicken together with the sesame seeds and chilli.
- Add the warm rice to the bowl and stir through the lime juice and oil. Season well and serve.

Chicken and Wild Rice Salad

134

- Use half white and half wild rice to add a nutty texture and extra substance.

135

Chicken and Vegetable Rice Salad

- Measure the rice (in volume) into a saucepan and cover with the stock. Cover with a lid and cook for 10 minutes.
- Remove from the heat and leave to sit for 5 minutes with the lid on. Then remove the lid and leave to cool a little in a bowl while you prepare the remaining salad ingredients.
- Mix the carrot, pepper, chicken and beansprouts in a bowl.
- Add the warm rice to the bowl and stir through the vinegar and oil. Season well and serve topped with coriander.

PREPARATION TIME 20 MINUTES

COOKING TIME 15 MINUTES

INGREDIENTS

240 ml / 8 ½ oz / 1 cup rice
480 ml / 1 pint / 2 cups weak chicken or vegetable stock
1 carrot, peeled and diced
1 green pepper, deseeded and finely chopped
2 chicken breasts, cooked and shredded
100 g / 3 ½ oz / ¾ cup beansprouts
2 tbsp white wine vinegar
4 tbsp olive oil
salt and pepper
coriander (cilantro) leaves to garnish

Chicken Salad with Courgettes   136

- Try adding sauteed courgettes (zucchini) to the mix for a different texture and colour.

137

SERVES 2

Chicken and Ginger Bites

- Marinate the chicken with the ginger, oil and lemon for at least 2 hours.
- Make the batter: whisk together the beer or water and the egg in a bowl until light and frothy.
- Whisk in the flour. You should have a light batter with a dropping consistency.
- Heat the oil to 180°C / 350F.
- Dip the chicken pieces a few at a time into the batter to coat thoroughly. Drop immediately into the hot oil. Do this in batches so as not to overcrowd the pan.
- Remove with a slotted spoon once golden-brown and drain on kitchen paper.
- Sprinkle with salt before serving and serve on lettuce leaves with soy sauce to dip and coriander to garnish.

PREPARATION TIME 10 MINUTES

COOKING TIME 15 MINUTES

INGREDIENTS

2 chicken thighs, skinned, deboned and cut into chunks
1 tbsp fresh ginger, grated
1 tbsp vegetable oil
2 tbsp lemon juice
vegetable oil, for deep-frying
salt
little gem lettuce leaves
soy sauce for dipping
coriander (cilantro) leaves to garnish

FOR THE BATTER
200 ml / 7 fl. oz / ¾ cup Japanese beer or lager or sparkling water
1 egg
100 g / 3 ½ oz / ½ cup plain (all purpose) flour

Spicy Ginger Bites   138

- Add a teaspoon of chilli (chili) powder to the batter for an extra kick.

Oat-crusted Chicken Meatballs

Meatballs with Hummus

140

- You can make a quick hummus by whizzing a can of drained chickpeas with tahini, crushed garlic, olive oil and lemon juice to serve with the meatballs.

Meatballs with Courgette

141

- Cut 2 courgettes (zucchini) into thin batons and fry slowly in olive oil with basil and lemon juice to finish.

PREPARATION TIME 25 MINUTES

COOKING TIME 40 MINUTES

INGREDIENTS

2 slices stale bread, crusts removed
1 kg / 2 ¼ lbs / 4 ¼ cups minced chicken
1 onion, peeled and grated
1 clove of garlic, crushed
1 lemon, juiced and zested
1 tsp dried oregano
salt and pepper
80 g / 2 ½ oz / ⅓ cup coarse oatmeal
100 ml / 3 ½ fl. oz / ½ cup olive oil
2 carrots, peeled and sliced
1 tbsp tahini
200 ml / 7 fl. oz / ¾ cup plain yoghurt
3 tbsp extra virgin olive oil

- Soak the bread in warm water then squeeze it out. Mix thoroughly with the meat, onions, garlic, zest and oregano and season carefully.

- Form into small balls around 6 cm in diameter. Roll in the oatmeal until coated all over. Refrigerate for 30 minutes.

- Meanwhile heat half the oil in a deep-sided pan and gently cook the carrots over a low / medium heat until tender and golden. Season and drizzle with a little lemon juice.

- Heat the remaining oil in a pan and fry the meatballs in batches until golden and cooked through.

- Stir the tahini through the yoghurt with the extra virgin olive oil and season carefully. Serve with the meatballs and carrots.

142 · SERVES 2 · Chicken Pittas with Avocado Salad

- Heat the oil in a pan and sauté the chicken and peppers over a high heat until golden and tender. Set aside to cool a little.
- Mix the mayonnaise with the spices, lemon juice and spring onions. Tip the chicken and peppers into the bowl and mix thoroughly.
- Warm and split the pitta breads and spoon the chicken mixture into the cavities.
- Halve, stone and scoop out the avocado flesh into a bowl, then add the remaining ingredients and mix well.
- Serve the pittas with the avocado salad alongside.

PREPARATION TIME 20 MINUTES

COOKING TIME 10 MINUTES

INGREDIENTS

2 tbsp olive oil
2 chicken breasts, chopped
2 red peppers, deseeded and roughly chopped
100 g / 3 ½ oz / ½ cup mayonnaise
2 tsp smoked paprika
1 tbsp lemon juice
½ tsp cayenne pepper
½ bunch spring onions (scallions), finely sliced
2 pitta breads

FOR THE SALAD
2 avocados
½ lemon, juiced
salt and pepper
2 tbsp extra virgin olive oil
2 tomatoes, cored and diced
1 tsp ground cumin

Chicken Pittas with Guacamole — 143

- Take this one step further and mash the avocado with the salad ingredients to make a lumpy mash. Spoon into the pitta breads with the chicken.

144 · SERVES 4–6 · Chicken and Prune Parcels

- Preheat the oven to 200°C (180°C fan) / 400F / gas 6.
- Heat the oil in a pan and cook the chicken, spices and prunes until cooked through. Set aside to cool.
- Keeping the remaining filo sheets covered with a damp tea towel, remove one at a time from the pack and brush with melted butter before using.
- Place 2 sheets of pastry on a surface, brush each with melted butter, then top with a little of the chicken mixture. Wrap the pastry around to enclose the filling. Repeat until all the filling and pastry is used up.
- Brush the tops with a little egg yolk, then bake in the oven for 15–20 minutes or until the pastry is crisp and golden.
- Serve hot.

PREPARATION TIME 20 MINUTES

COOKING TIME 30 MINUTES

INGREDIENTS

4 tbsp olive oil
2 chicken breasts, skinned and diced
½ tsp ground cinnamon
½ tsp ground cumin
½ tsp ground coriander (cilantro)
100 g / 3 ½ oz / ½ cup prunes, chopped
salt and pepper
1 pack filo pastry
120 g / 4 oz / ½ cup butter, melted
1 egg yolk, beaten

Savoury Chicken Parcels — 145

- Try using diced cooked potato in place of the prunes for a more substantial parcel.

146

SERVES 4–6

Chicken Croquettes with Tomato Sauce

PREPARATION TIME 30 MINUTES

COOKING TIME 30 MINUTES

INGREDIENTS

1.5 kg / 3 lb / 6 cups floury potatoes,
peeled and quartered
50 g / 1 ¾ oz / ¼ cup butter
4 egg yolks, beaten
2 chicken breasts, cooked and
shredded finely
¼ bunch parsley, finely chopped
salt and pepper
2 tbsp olive oil
1 clove of garlic, finely chopped
400 g / 14 oz / 1 ½ cups canned
tomatoes
½ bunch basil, chopped
6 tbsp flour
2 eggs, beaten
200 g / 7 oz / ¾ cup breadcrumbs,
to coat
vegetable oil, for deep frying

- Cook the potatoes in boiling water until tender. Drain, then return to the pan and allow to dry.
- Mash the potatoes with the butter until smooth. Work in the egg yolks, then season and add the chicken and parsley. Spread the mash in a greased dish and leave to cool.
- Meanwhile heat the olive oil in a pan and when very hot, add the garlic and tomatoes. Cover immediately with a lid and cook fast for 10 minutes. Remove the lid, stir in the basil and seasoning and set aside.
- Lightly flour your hands, then work the cooled mixture into a ball. Shape into a long cylinder and cut into 5 cm logs. Dip each croquette into the flour, egg and then the breadcrumbs to coat.
- Heat the oil to 180°C / 350F. Deep fry the croquettes in batches until golden-brown. Drain on kitchen paper and serve hot with the sauce.

Chicken Croquettes

147

- You can add any kind of flavouring. Vary the herbs, add curry powder or chilli, the choice is endless.

148

SERVES 4

Chicken, Orange and Pepper Kebabs

PREPARATION TIME 10 MINUTES

COOKING TIME 10 MINUTES

INGREDIENTS

4 chicken breasts, skinned
2 tbsp thyme leaves
2 tbsp olive oil
salt and pepper
2 oranges, thinly sliced
1 red pepper, deseeded and chopped
1 green pepper, deseeded and
chopped
1 yellow pepper, deseeded and
chopped

- Cut the chicken into large cubes and tip into a bowl with the thyme, oil, salt and pepper and mix well.
- Thread onto soaked wooden skewers, alternating with folded slices of orange and pieces of pepper.
- Griddle or barbecue over medium heat for 10 minutes or so, turning every so often, until golden and cooked through.
- Serve hot.

Chicken and Orange Kebabs with Almond Crust

149

- Try rolling the cooked kebabs in 2 tbsp ground almonds for added texture.

150

SERVES 2–4

Chicken Wings with Ginger

Chicken Thighs with Ginger

151

- Replace the chicken wings with chicken thighs.

Chicken Wings with Soy

152

- If cola does not appeal, use 3–4 tbsp soy sauce instead.

PREPARATION TIME 1 HOUR

COOKING TIME 30–40 MINUTES

INGREDIENTS

8–12 chicken wings
200 ml / 7 fl. oz / ¾ cup full-fat cola
1 tbsp black peppercorns, crushed
1 bunch spring onions (scallions), chopped
1 tbsp fresh ginger, grated
1 tsp salt

- Marinate the chicken wings with the rest of the ingredients for at least 1 hour.
- Preheat the oven to 200°C (180°C fan) / 400F / gas 6.
- Tip the chicken wings and the spring onions into a foil-lined roasting tin, reserving the marinade and roast for 30–40 minutes until the wings are sticky and dark gold.
- Pour the remaining marinade into a small pan and reduce until syrupy. Taste and adjust the seasoning if necessary – you may want more salt or even a squeeze of lime juice.
- Serve the chicken wings and spring onions with the reduced sauce spooned over.

153

MAKES 12

Chicken and Tomato Crostini

PREPARATION TIME 20 MINUTES

COOKING TIME 20 MINUTES

INGREDIENTS

4 chicken breasts, skin on
12 x 1 cm (½ in) thick slices from a baguette
3 tbsp olive oil
6 ripe vine tomatoes
6 tbsp mayonnaise
salt and pepper

- Preheat the oven to 200°C (180°C fan) / 400F / gas 6.
- Drizzle the chicken with a little oil, season and roast in the oven for 20 minutes or until just cooked through. Set aside to rest.
- Brush the baguette slices with a little oil and bake in the oven for 10–12 minutes until crisp and golden.
- Finely dice the tomatoes, coring them first, then toss with the mayonnaise and season generously.
- Slice the chicken breasts. Spoon the tomatoes on top of the crostini and top with chicken.

Spicy Chicken Tomato Crostini

154

- Spice up the mayonnaise with mango chutney, paprika, herbs or mustard. The choice is yours.

155

SERVES 6–8

Chicken and Swiss Chard Terrine

PREPARATION TIME 30 MINUTES

COOKING TIME 45 MINUTES

INGREDIENTS

100 g / 3 ½ oz / ½ cup butter
2 shallots, finely chopped
1 clove of garlic, crushed
2 sprigs thyme
500 g / 1 lb / 2 cups minced chicken
500 g / 1 lb / 2 cups chicken meat, diced
2 tbsp tarragon leaves, chopped (optional)
2 eggs + 2 egg yolks, lightly beaten
salt and pepper
1 kg / 2 lb / 4 cups Swiss chard leaves

- Preheat the oven to 160°C (140°C fan) / 325F / gas 3.
- Heat the butter in a pan and sweat the shallot and garlic with the thyme until softened. Set aside to cool.
- In a large bowl, mix together the chicken and tarragon with the shallot mixture once cooled. Add the beaten eggs, then season.
- Steam the Swiss chard leaves for 3–4 minutes, then pat dry. Finely chop a few leaves and reserve.
- Line a terrine mould with film and layer the chard leaves so they overlap. Spoon half the chicken mixture in, top with the chopped chard, then the remaining chicken, then fold the chard leaves over to cover.
- Cover the terrine with greaseproof paper, then foil and secure with string. Place in a roasting tin and fill with boiling water to halfway up the sides of the mould.
- Bake in the oven for 45 minutes.
- Leave to cool in the mould, then remove and slice.

Chicken and Mushroom Terrine

156

- Try adding 250 g / 9 oz / 1 cup mixed wild mushrooms to the shallot mixture for extra flavour.

157

SERVES 4

Chicken Kebabs with Apricots

- Tip the chicken and apricot halves into a bowl and leave to marinate with the remaining ingredients for 30–60 minutes.
- Thread the chicken, spring onions and apricots alternately onto soaked wooden skewers and griddle or barbecue over a medium heat until golden and cooked through.
- Serve hot or warm.

PREPARATION TIME 10 MINUTES
+ MARINATING TIME

COOKING TIME 10 MINUTES

INGREDIENTS

4 chicken thighs, skinned, deboned and chopped
4 ripe apricots, halved and stoned
½ bunch thyme
2 tbsp olive oil
salt and pepper
½ lemon, zested
1 bunch spring onions (scallions), sliced

Chicken with Plums

158

- Plums work just as well for a late summer barbecue. Try adding a little chopped chilli for kick or hoisin sauce.

159

SERVES 2

Exotic Chicken Salad

- Preheat the oven to 200°C (180°C fan) / 400F / gas 6.
- Drizzle the chicken with olive oil, season and roast in the oven for 20 minutes or until cooked through. Set aside to rest.
- Meanwhile mix the pineapple, tomatoes and cucumber in a bowl. Rinse, dry and arrange the salad leaves in a serving bowl.
- Whisk together the extra virgin olive oil, lime juice and zest, chilli and a little salt, then combine well with the diced fruit. Drizzle on top of the salad leaves.
- Thickly slice the chicken, arrange on top of the fruit and serve.

PREPARATION TIME 15 MINUTES

COOKING TIME 20 MINUTES

INGREDIENTS

2 chicken breasts, skin on
2 tbsp olive oil
salt and pepper
½ pineapple, peeled, cored and diced
2 ripe vine tomatoes, cored and diced
½ cucumber, diced
300 g / 10 oz / 1 ¼ cups Mesclun salad
80 ml / 2 ½ fl. oz / ⅓ cup extra virgin olive oil
1 lime, juiced and zested
½ red chilli (chili), finely chopped

Exotic Salad with Mango

160

- Try adding diced mango, which goes really well with the chilli, and cooked prawns.

161

SERVES 4

Chicken Tandoori Brochettes

PREPARATION TIME 10 MINUTES
+ MARINATING TIME

COOKING TIME 8–10 MINUTES

....

INGREDIENTS

4 skinless chicken breasts,
cut into thin strips

FOR THE MARINADE
300 ml / 10 fl. oz / 1 ¼ cups plain
yoghurt
1 tsp ground cumin
1 tsp ground coriander (cilantro)
1 tsp garam masala
1 tsp ground cinnamon
1 ½ tsp tandoori chilli (chili) powder
1 tsp paprika
1 tsp caster (superfine) sugar
1 clove garlic, minced
salt and pepper

- Prepare the tandoori marinade by mixing together
  all the ingredients for the marinade in a mixing bowl.
  Add the chicken, mix well, then cover and chill for at
  least 1 hour.
- Pre-heat the grill to hot. Remove the chicken from
  the marinade, shaking off any excess, and thread
  onto soaked wooden skewers.
- Grill for 8–10 minutes, turning occasionally until
  lightly charred and cooked through.

Curried Chicken Kebabs   162

- Try marinating in any kind of curry
  paste such as masala, korma or even
  mango chutney with lime zest.

163

SERVES 8

Chicken and Prawn Open Sandwiches

PREPARATION TIME 20 MINUTES

....

INGREDIENTS

16 slices baguette, about 2 cm (1 in)
thick
2 chicken breasts, cooked and diced
200 g / 7 oz / ¾ cup cooked king
prawns
100 g / 3 ½ oz / ½ cup mayonnaise
½ lemon, juiced
salt and pepper
salad leaves and lemon zest, to
garnish

- Place the baguette slices on a baking sheet and grill
  until lightly toasted.
- Mix the chicken with the prawns, mayonnaise, a
  squeeze of lemon and seasoning and combine well.
- Pile the mixture onto the baguette slices and serve
  topped with salad leaves and a sprinkle of lemon zest.

Smoked Fish and Chicken   164
Open Sandwiches

- Add smoked mackerel or salmon with the
  prawns and mayonnaise.

165

SERVES 2

Steamed Lemon Chicken Salad

Lemon Chicken Rice Paper Rolls

 166

- If you shred the steamed chicken finely, you could use it and the salad as a filler for rice paper rolls to serve as a starter.

Vietnamese Ginger Steamed Chicken

 167

- Use 2 cm piece of fresh ginger, finely sliced, pushed under the chicken in the steaming process.

PREPARATION TIME 10 MINUTES

COOKING TIME 20–25 MINUTES

INGREDIENTS

2 chicken breasts, skinned
1 tbsp fish sauce
3 stalks lemongrass, bruised
1 lemon, sliced
1 red chilli (chili), chopped
2 cloves of garlic, sliced
250 g / 9 oz / 1 cup rocket (arugula)
1 bunch radishes, tailed and sliced
1 bunch spring onions (scallions), sliced
30 g / 1 oz / ¼ cup peanuts, chopped

- Place a steamer or muslin-lined colander over a pan of simmering water and place in it the lemongrass, lemon slices, chilli and garlic. Sit the chicken on top, sprinkle over the fish sauce, put on the lid and steam for 20–25 minutes until cooked through.

- Meanwhile toss together the rocket, radishes and spring onions in a bowl ready for serving.

- When the chicken is cooked, remove from the steamer, slice and sit on top of the salad with the ingredients from the steamer and the peanuts scattered over.

168

SERVES 2

Chicken, Fig and Mange Tout Salad

Crunchy Chicken and Fig Salad

169

- Add pistachios, pine nuts or cashews for crunch and texture.

Chicken Fig Salad with Pomegranate

170

- Add 1 tsp pomegranate molasses or even honey to the dressing.

PREPARATION TIME 10 MINUTES

COOKING TIME 4 MINUTES

INGREDIENTS

2 chicken breasts, roasted and cooled
4 figs, quartered
100 g / 3 ½ oz / ½ cup mange tout
1 shallot, finely chopped
2 tbsp extra virgin olive oil
½ lemon, juiced
salt and pepper
2 tbsp basil leaves, shredded

- Finely slice the chicken and toss with the figs in a bowl.
- Steam the mange tout over simmering water until tender—about 4 minutes.
- Whisk the shallot with the oil, lemon, basil and salt and pepper.
- Toss the mange tout with the chicken then coat in the dressing and serve.

171

SERVES 4

Chicken Caesar Salad with Grapefruit

- Thickly slice the chicken breasts and set aside.
- Tip the salad leaves into a serving bowl with the raw pepper. Steam the baby sweetcorn for about 4 minutes until tender then add to the bowl.
- Cut away the skin of the grapefruit, using the knife to follow the fruit down the sides, cutting away the white pith as well as the skin. Segment into a bowl to catch any juice, then add the grapefruit segments to the salad bowl and toss gently to combine.
- For the dressing, mash the anchovy fillets with the garlic to a pulp, then stir in the crème fraîche, lemon juice and Parmesan and season carefully. You may want more lemon juice.
- Add 2 tbsp of the dressing to the salad and coat thoroughly.
- Add the chicken to the salad then spoon over the remaining dressing.

Chicken Caesar with Soft-boiled Egg

172

- Add quarters of soft-boiled egg and a tbsp of drained capers for a very grown-up version.

PREPARATION TIME 15 MINUTES

COOKING TIME 5 MINUTES

INGREDIENTS

2 chicken breasts, skinned and roasted or bought pre-cooked
200 g / 7 oz / ¾ cup mixed salad leaves
1 red pepper, deseeded and finely sliced
100 g / 3 ½ oz / ½ cup baby sweetcorn
1 grapefruit

FOR THE DRESSING

2 anchovy fillets
½ clove of garlic, crushed
150 ml / 5 fl. oz / ⅔ cup crème fraîche
squeeze of lemon juice
2–3 tbsp Parmesan, grated
salt and pepper

173

SERVES 4–6

Mini Chicken Liver Terrines

- Heat a tbsp of butter in a frying pan and cook the chicken livers over a medium heat for 5 minutes, turning them frequently, until golden brown without and just pink within.
- Transfer with a slotted spoon to a food processor, reserving the frying pan and juices.
- Pour the alcohol into the pan, scraping with a wooden spoon, reduce by half and add to the processor.
- Melt 150 g butter and pour into the processor. Add the mace, thyme, garlic and salt and pepper. Blend to a smooth puree.
- Spoon into individual ramekins. Melt the remaining butter and pour over, leave to cool then chill for 24 hours before scattering with hazelnuts and serving with hot toast.

PREPARATION TIME 20 MINUTES
+ CHILLING TIME

COOKING TIME 10 MINUTES

INGREDIENTS

225 g / 8 oz / 1 cup chicken livers, trimmed
225 g / 8 oz / 1 cup butter, softened
75 ml / 2 ½ fl. oz / ⅓ cup madeira or marsala
¼ tsp ground mace
1 tsp thyme leaves
1 clove of garlic, crushed
salt and pepper
chopped toasted hazelnuts (cob nuts)

Chicken Liver and Caper Terrines

174

- The sharpness of capers nicely offset the richness, so try adding 1 tbsp drained capers to the mix after processing.

175 **SERVES 4**

Chicken Wings with Lemon and Thyme

PREPARATION TIME 10 MINUTES

COOKING TIME 35–40 MINUTES

INGREDIENTS

16 chicken wings
100 g / 3 ½ oz / ½ cup butter
1 lemon, juiced
¼ bunch thyme
salt and pepper

- Preheat the oven to 200°C (180°C fan) / 400F / gas 6.
- Melt the butter in a pan and add the lemon, thyme and seasoning. Brush over the chicken wings and coat thoroughly.
- Place the chicken wings in a roasting tin and roast in the oven for 20 minutes. Turn them over, brush again with the butter then roast for another 15–20 minutes until sticky, golden and cooked through.
- Serve hot.

Chicken Wings with Rosemary 176

- Use rosemary sprigs to brush on the butter to add extra herby flavour.

177 **SERVES 4**

Chicken Rice Salad

PREPARATION TIME 25 MINUTES

COOKING TIME 20 MINUTES

INGREDIENTS

250 g / 9 oz / 1 cup basmati rice, cooked and cooled
2 chicken breasts, skin on
3 tbsp groundnut oil
1 tsp Chinese 5-spice powder
1 red pepper, deseeded and finely diced
1 green pepper, deseeded and finely diced
1 carrot, peeled and diagonally sliced
2-3 tbsp rice vinegar
salt and pepper
1 tsp sugar
1 tbsp chopped pecan nuts, toasted
few sprigs coriander (cilantro)

- Preheat the oven to 200°C (180°C fan) / 400F / gas 6.
- Rub the chicken with 2 tbsp oil and 5-spice and roast in the oven for 20 minutes until cooked. Set aside to rest.
- Mix the cooled rice with the peppers and carrot. Whisk together the rice vinegar, oil, seasoning and a little sugar, taste and correct the seasoning. Toss with the rice.
- Slice the chicken into chunks and sit on top of the rice salad with the pecans. Decorate with sprigs of coriander and serve.

Chicken Soy Rice Salad 178

- For a more savoury flavour, add 1 tbsp soy sauce to the dressing.

179

SERVES 4

Chicken Fajitas

Chicken Fajitas with Rice

 180

- Serve alongside Mexican spiced rice.

Chicken Tacos

 181

- Use the crisp boat-shape tacos for a change to tortilla wraps.

PREPARATION TIME 35 MINUTES

COOKING TIME 10–15 MINUTES

INGREDIENTS

4 chicken breasts, skinned and thinly sliced
2 tsp paprika
2 tsp ground cumin
2 tsp ground coriander (cilantro)
pinch dried chilli (chili) flakes
salt and pepper
4 tbsp olive oil
1 onion, peeled and finely sliced
1 red pepper, deseeded and finely sliced
3 stalks celery, sliced
1 courgette (zucchini), cut into batons
1 lime, juiced
8 tortilla wraps
sour cream, tomato salsa and guacamole to serve

- Coat the chicken in half the spices and leave to marinate for 30 minutes.
- Heat half the oil in a pan until nearly smoking, then cook the onion, peppers, celery and courgettes until golden and tender. Remove from the pan, keep warm and set aside.
- Add the remaining oil to the pan and reheat, then add the chicken and sprinkle over the remaining spices.
- Stir briskly for 2–3 minutes until the chicken is just cooked through. Squeeze over the lime juice. Remove and keep warm.
- Wipe out the pan and use to warm the tortillas through.
- Serve the vegetables with the meat, tortilla wraps and sauces.

182

SERVES 4

Chicken with Saffron Rice

PREPARATION TIME 10 MINUTES

COOKING TIME 30 MINUTES

INGREDIENTS

4 chicken legs
2 tbsp runny honey
2 tbsp grain mustard
2 tbsp vegetable oil
salt and pepper
1 onion, peeled and finely diced
1 courgette (zucchini), diced
2 tomatoes, cored and diced
250 g / 9 oz / 1 cup basmati rice
480 ml / 16 fl. oz / 2 cups water
infused with pinch saffron

- Preheat the oven to 190°C (170°C fan) / 375F / gas 5.
- Mix together the honey, mustard, half the oil and seasoning and coat the chicken. Roast in a foil-lined tray for 30 minutes or until golden and sticky.
- Tip the rice into a pan with the water and cook covered with a lid for 10 minutes. Remove from the heat and leave covered for 5 minutes.
- Sauté the onion and courgette briefly in the remaining oil then add to the rice with the tomatoes. Fork through.
- Serve the chicken with the rice alongside.

Sticky Chicken Pittas

183

- This would sit well in split warmed pitta breads for a lunchtime treat.

184

SERVES 6

Chicken and Goats' Cheese Ravioli

PREPARATION TIME 45 MINUTES

COOKING TIME 3 MINUTES

INGREDIENTS

FOR THE PASTA
500g / 1 lb / 2 cups '00' flour
6 eggs
butter
Parmesan, grated

FOR THE FILLING
200 g / 7 oz / ¾ cup chicken breast, cooked and finely shredded
100 g / 3 ½ oz / ½ cup goats' cheese, chopped
100 g / 3 ½ oz / ½ cup ricotta
8 chive stalks, finely chopped
salt and pepper

- Place the flour in a bowl and make a well in the centre. Crack the eggs into the well. Beat the eggs, then draw in the flour a little at a time to form a dough.
- Remove the dough from the bowl and knead for 5 minutes. Cover with clingfilm and refrigerate for 30 minutes.
- Meanwhile make the filling: Mix together all the ingredients until thoroughly combined.
- Remove the pasta from the fridge. Roll out the dough on a floured surface to 1–2 mm thick. Use a 6 cm (2 ½ in) fluted cutter to stamp out rounds.
- Place a heaped tsp of filling in the middle of each circle.
- Fold each circle in half to enclose the filling. Press down gently to push out the air. Press the edges together to seal tightly.
- Bring a pan of water to the boil and cook for 3 minutes. Remove then toss with butter and Parmesan cheese.

Spinach, Ricotta and Chicken Ravioli

185

- Add 300 g / 10 oz / 1 ½ cups wilted spinach, squeezed dry, for a different flavour.

186

SERVES 2

Grilled Chicken and Spring Vegetables

Spring Vegetable Salad

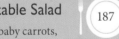

187

- Try scrubbed baby carrots, quartered fennel bulbs, or halved baby beetroot for variation.

Chicken and Spring Vegetable Pasta

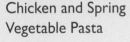

188

- Serve tossed with cooked fusilli pasta.

PREPARATION TIME 15 MINUTES

COOKING TIME 20 MINUTES

·······

INGREDIENTS

2 chicken breasts, skin on
1 tbsp olive oil
salt and pepper
100 g / 3 ½ oz / ½ cup broad beans
1 bunch asparagus, trimmed
2 ripe tomatoes, cut into wedges
3 tbsp extra virgin olive oil
½ lemon, juiced
bunch fresh parsley, chopped

- Rub the chicken with oil and seasoning and cook on a griddle pan over medium heat skin side down until golden and crisp. Turn over and cook on the other side for 4 minutes or until cooked through. Set aside to rest.

- Meanwhile cook the beans in salted boiling water for 4 minutes, then drain. Pop the broad beans out of their grey shells; discard the shells and tip the beans into a bowl.

- Steam the asparagus spears over simmering water for 3-4 minutes until tender to the point of a knife. Cut into short lengths and add to the bowl with the tomatoes.

- Whisk the oil, lemon juice and parsley seasoning together and toss the vegetables in it gently.

- Slice the chicken and serve with the salad.

189

SERVES 4

Chicken, Raisin and Almond Salad

PREPARATION TIME 15 MINUTES

COOKING TIME 15 MINUTES

INGREDIENTS

4 chicken breasts, skin on
1 tbsp olive oil
salt and pepper
80 g / 2 ½ oz / ⅓ cup raisins
80 g / 2 ½ oz / ⅓ cup whole almonds, skinned
2 heads red chicory, leaves separated
2 tsp honey
1 tbsp grain mustard
60 ml / 2 fl. oz / ¼ cup extra virgin olive oil
few thyme sprigs

- Rub the chicken with oil and seasoning and cook on a griddle pan over medium heat skin side down until golden and crisp. Turn over and cook on the other side for 4 minutes or until cooked through. Set aside to rest.
- Place the almonds, raisins and chicory in a serving bowl.
- Whisk together the honey and mustard, then whisk in the extra virgin olive oil to make an emulsion. Season.
- Slice the chicken and sit on top of the salad. Spoon over the dressing, scatter with thyme and serve.

Chicken Orange Almond Salad

190

- Add orange segments and use a drop of rosewater in the dressing for a hint of the Middle East.

191

SERVES 2

Salmon Sauce and Chicken Sauce

PREPARATION TIME 20 MINUTES

COOKING TIME 25 MINUTES

INGREDIENTS

FOR THE CHICKEN SAUCE
30 g / 1 oz butter
1 shallot, finely chopped
1 clove of garlic, finely chopped
2 chicken thighs, skinned, deboned and chopped
100 ml / 3 ½ fl. oz / ½ cup white wine
200 ml / 7 fl. oz / ¾ cup creme fraîche
few sprigs chervil
salt and pepper

FOR THE SALMON SAUCE
30 g / 1 oz butter
1 shallot, finely chopped
100 ml / 3 ½ fl. oz / ½ cup white wine
200 ml / 7 fl. oz / ¾ cup creme fraîche
200 g / 7 oz / ¾ cup smoked salmon trimmings
½ lemon, juiced
4 king prawns, cooked
lemon zest, to garnish

- Make the chicken sauce: Heat the butter in a pan and sweat the shallot and garlic without colouring. Increase the heat slightly, add the chicken and cook until golden.
- Add the white wine, reduce by half then stir in the creme fraîche and chervil. Season and serve.
- Make the salmon sauce: Heat the butter in a pan and sweat the shallot without colouring. Add the white wine, reduce by half, then add the creme fraîche.
- When hot, stir in the salmon, season and add a squeeze of lemon juice. Stir in the prawns and serve garnished with lemon zest.

Pasta with Salmon Sauce and Chicken Sauce

192

- Boil 2 portions of pasta, according to the packet instructions. Toss the pasta in the sauce and serve.

193

SERVES 4

Chicken and Grapefruit Salad

- Shred or finely slice the chicken and place in a bowl.
- Segment the grapefruit holding it over a bowl then squeeze any excess juice into the bowl as well. Tip the segments in with the chicken.
- Whisk the grapefruit juice with the oil and some seasoning.
- Add the lettuce leaves, onion, artichokes and walnuts to the chicken and toss everything lightly in the dressing, then serve sprinkled with chives.

PREPARATION TIME 20 MINUTES

INGREDIENTS

4 chicken breasts, cooked
1 grapefruit, peeled
3 tbsp extra virgin olive oil
salt and pepper
1 head little gem lettuce, leaves separated
1 red onion, peeled and finely sliced
4 cooked artichoke hearts from a jar, sliced
2 tbsp walnuts, crushed
fresh chopped chives

Chicken and Blood Orange Salad

194

- This would work well with blood oranges in season, or try normal oranges pepped up with a little lime or lemon juice.

195

SERVES 4

Chicken Nuggets with Tartare Sauce

- Bash the chicken breasts between 2 pieces clingfilm with a rolling pin until about 2 cm thick.
- Cut each piece into thick strips and place in a bowl with the buttermilk. Refrigerate for at least 2 hours or even overnight.
- To make the sauce, mix the mayonnaise with the rest of the ingredients. Taste, adjust the seasoning and chill until needed.
- The next day, dip the chicken strips one at a time into the flour, egg then breadcrumbs mixed with the flavourings and lay on a rack to dry slightly.
- Heat 1 cm depth oil in a pan and fry the chicken in batches until golden on both sides and cooked through.
- Serve with the sauce on the side to dunk.

PREPARATION TIME 20 MINUTES
+ MARINATING TIME

COOKING TIME 15 MINUTES

INGREDIENTS

4 chicken breasts, skinned
300 ml / 10 fl. oz / 1 ¼ cups buttermilk
100 g / 3 ½ oz / ½ cup plain (all purpose) flour
2 eggs, beaten
200 g / 7 oz / ¾ cup breadcrumbs
1 tsp mustard powder
pinch cayenne
vegetable oil

FOR THE SAUCE
200 g / 7 oz / ¾ cup mayonnaise
1 shallot, finely chopped
2 gherkins or cornichons, chopped
2 tbsp capers, drained
½ bunch parsley, chopped
½ lemon, juiced
salt and pepper

Chicken Nuggets and Spicy Sauce

196

- Try mixing tomato ketchup, Dijon mustard, lime pickle and Worcestershire sauce in a small bowl, to achieve a dipping sauce for nuggets.

CLASSIC MAINS

197

SERVES 4

Tapenade Chicken with Sautéed Potatoes

PREPARATION TIME 10 MINUTES

COOKING TIME 30 MINUTES

....

INGREDIENTS

80 g / 2 ½ oz / ⅓ cup black olive
tapenade
4 chicken breasts, skinned
salt and pepper
olive oil
1 kg / 2 lb / 4 cups waxy potatoes,
quartered
1 kg / 2 lb / 4 cups baby spinach
leaves, washed
½ lemon, juiced

- Preheat the oven to 200°C (180°C fan) / 400F / gas 6.
- Rub the tapenade over the chicken breasts, then place in a roasting tin, drizzle with a little oil and cook for 20–30 minutes, until cooked through.
- Heat 4 tbsp olive oil in a deep-sided pan and cook the potatoes, turning occasionally, until crisp and cooked through. Season.
- Toss the spinach leaves with a little oil, lemon juice and seasoning.
- Serve the chicken thighs with the potatoes and spinach leaves.

Sun-dried Tomato Tapenade Chicken

198

- You could use sun-dried tomato or normal pesto in place of the tapenade.

199

SERVES 4

Poached Chicken with Chanterelles

PREPARATION TIME 10 MINUTES

COOKING TIME 45 MINUTES

....

INGREDIENTS

4 chicken breasts, skin removed
1 celery stick, chopped
1 carrot, chopped
½ onion
6 black peppercorns
1 bay leaf
50 g / 1 ¾ oz / ¼ cup butter
50 g / 1 ¾ oz / ¼ cup plain
(all purpose) flour
100 ml / 3 ½ fl. oz / ½ cup double
(heavy) cream
salt and pepper
40 g / 1 oz butter
100 g / 3 ½ oz / ½ cup chanterelle
mushrooms, brushed

- Place the chicken in a pan with the vegetables, peppercorns and bay leaf. Cover with water, simmer and skim any scum from the top.
- Leave to poach at barely a 'blip' for about 20 minutes, or until just cooked through. Remove the chicken from the pan, then strain and reserve the poaching liqour.
- Melt 50 g butter in a pan and stir in the flour to make a paste. Slowly whisk in 300 ml of the poaching liquid to make a smooth thick sauce. Season and leave to simmer gently for about 10 minutes to cook out the flour.
- Meanwhile melt 40 g butter in a pan and sauté the mushrooms until just cooked.
- Stir the cream into the velouté and adjust the seasoning. Spoon over the chicken with the mushrooms.

Poached Chicken with Courgettes

200

- Try sautéing diced courgettes to serve alongside when chanterelles are not in season.

201

SERVES 4

Creamy Chicken

- Preheat the oven to 220°C (200°C fan) / 425F / gas 7.
- Season the chicken pieces, then dredge lightly in flour.
- Heat a little oil in a pan with the butter and sauté the chicken until golden brown on all sides. Transfer the pan to the oven and cook for a further 10–15 minutes or until cooked through.
- Remove the chicken to a dish and place the pan back on the heat. Add the shallots and cook until softened, then add the white wine, stirring to deglaze the pan.
- When reduced by two thirds, add the mushrooms, tarragon and chicken stock and reduce by half. Whisk in the cream, adjust the seasoning and cook until thickened.
- Serve the sauce over the chicken.

Creamy Chicken
with Crème Fraîche

202

- Try using crème fraîche instead of cream for a fresher tasting sauce.

PREPARATION TIME 10 MINUTES

COOKING TIME 35–40 MINUTES

....

INGREDIENTS

4 chicken pieces, skin on
salt and pepper
2 tbsp plain (all purpose) flour
olive oil
50 g / 1 ¾ oz / ¼ cup butter
2 shallots, finely chopped
100 g / 3 ½ oz / ½ cup button mushrooms
2 sprigs tarragon
200 ml / 7 fl. oz / ¾ cup dry white wine
200 ml / 7 fl. oz / ¾ cup chicken stock
75 ml / 2 ½ fl. oz / ⅓ cup double (heavy) cream

203

SERVES 4

Slow Cooked Chicken Etouffee

- Heat the oil in a deep sided pan and fry the chicken on all sides until golden.
- Add the onion and garlic with the bacon and continue to cook until deep gold and sweet.
- Meanwhile blanch the broad beans in boiling water for 4 minutes. Drain, cool slightly then pop out of the grey skins to leave the bright green beans.
- Add the potatoes and fennel to the chicken and cook for a few minutes, then add the thyme, beans and wine, season and cover with a lid.
- Cook over a low heat for 20–25 minutes until the chicken is cooked through.
- Serve with crusty bread.

Etouffee with Spring Vegetables

204

- Add baby turnips, peas, baby carrots and courgettes (zucchini) to ring the changes.

PREPARATION TIME 10 MINUTES

COOKING TIME 45–50 MINUTES

....

INGREDIENTS

2 tbsp olive oil
4 chicken legs
1 onion, peeled and finely sliced
2 cloves of garlic, finely sliced
4 rashers smoked streaky bacon, diced
200 g / 7 oz / ¾ cup broad beans
1 bulb fennel, cored and thickly sliced
8 waxy potatoes, quartered lengthways
4 sprigs thyme
200 ml / 7 fl. oz / ¾ cup white wine
salt and pepper

205

SERVES 4

Chicken and Apricot Tagine

Chicken Tagine with Dates

 206

- Replace the apricots with 150 g / 4 ½ oz / 1 cup stoned, chopped dates for a sweeter taste.

Chicken and Plum Tagine

 207

- In autumn, use halved stoned fresh plums in season.

PREPARATION TIME 10 MINUTES

COOKING TIME 45 MINUTES

INGREDIENTS

2 tbsp olive oil
1 onion, peeled and finely sliced
2 cloves of garlic, finely sliced
4 chicken thighs, skinned
1 tsp ras-el-hanout spice mix
1 tsp ground coriander (cilantro)
1 large pinch dried chilli (chili) flakes
400 ml / 14 fl. oz / 1 ½ cups chicken stock
200 g / 7 oz / ¾ cup dried apricots
100 g / 3 ½ oz / ¾ cup whole almonds
salt and pepper
basmati rice, cooked, to serve

- Heat the oil in a large pan and cook the onions until golden and tender.
- Add the garlic and cook for a few minutes, then remove all from the pan with a slotted spoon.
- Increase the heat and brown the chicken thighs on all sides, then tip the onions back into the pan and sprinkle over the spices.
- Pour over the stock, add the apricots and almonds and season, lower the heat and cook gently for about 45 minutes or until the sauce has thickened and the chicken is cooked.
- Serve with the basmati rice.

West Indian Roast Chicken

SERVES 4–6 — 208

- Preheat the oven to 220°C (200°C fan) / 425F / gas 7.
- Place the chicken in a roasting tin and stuff the cavity with the celery and herbs. Rub the breast with butter and season. Roast in the oven for 20 minutes.
- Reduce the heat to 180°C (160°C fan) / 350F / gas 4.
- Roast for 30 minutes then add the pineapple, sugar and the spices and cook for another 30–40 minutes or until the juices run clear when the thickest part of the chicken is pierced with a toothpick.
- Leave to rest for 20 minutes before carving and serve with the spiced pineapple.

Roast Chicken with Oranges — 209

- Replace the slices of pineapple with oranges.

PREPARATION TIME 10 MINUTES

**COOKING TIME
1 HOUR 30 MINUTES**

INGREDIENTS

1 oven ready chicken
3 sticks celery, chopped in half
small bunch thyme
2 bay leaves
salt and pepper
2 tbsp butter
1 cinnamon stick
2 star anise
½ pineapple, peeled and sliced into thick rings
1 tsp brown sugar

Roast Chicken with Persillade Tomatoes

SERVES 4–6 — 210

- Preheat the oven to 220°C (200°C fan) / 425F / gas 7.
- Place the chicken in a roasting tin, smear with oil and season generously, stuff the cavity with rosemary. Roast in the oven for 20 minutes.
- Reduce the heat to 180°C (160°C fan) / 350F / gas 4 and cook for 1 hour or until the juices run clear when pierced with a toothpick. Leave to rest for 20 minutes.
- Meanwhile, place the parsley, garlic, 1 tsp salt and zest on a board and very finely chop with a sharp knife. Sprinkle on top of the tomatoes and place in a roasting tin. Roast in the oven for 15 minutes until tender.
- Serve the chicken carved with the persillade tomatoes alongside.

Roast Chicken with Balsamic Tomatoes — 211

- Drizzle balsamic vinegar over the tomatoes for an extra tang.

PREPARATION TIME 10 MINUTES

**COOKING TIME
1 HOUR 30 MINUTES**

INGREDIENTS

4 ripe tomatoes, halved
2 tbsp olive oil
salt and pepper
1 oven ready chicken
3 sprigs rosemary
1 bunch parsley, chopped
2 cloves of garlic, chopped
zest of 1 lemon

212

SERVES 4

Chicken and Pea Pie

PREPARATION TIME 30 MINUTES

COOKING TIME 25 MINUTES

INGREDIENTS

40 g / 1 oz butter
4 chicken thighs, skinned, deboned and chopped
150 g / 5 oz / ⅔ cup pancetta or diced streaky bacon
200 g / 7 oz / ¾ cup chestnut mushrooms, quartered
1 clove of garlic, finely chopped
250 g / 9 oz / 1 cup peas
350 ml / 12 fl. oz / 1 ½ cups double (heavy) cream
4 sprigs tarragon or thyme
salt and pepper
1 sheet ready rolled puff pastry
1 egg, beaten

- Preheat the oven to 190°C (170°C fan) / 375F / gas 5.
- Heat the butter in a pan and fry the chicken and bacon until golden and the fat starts to run.
- Add the mushrooms and garlic and cook until the liquid evaporates, then add the peas, cream and herbs, season and bubble up to thicken.
- Tip into a pie dish. Roll out the pastry on a floured surface, then place carefully over the pie filling.
- Brush with beaten egg and bake for 25 minutes or until the pastry is golden and risen.

Mini Chicken and Pea Pies 213

- If you have little gratin dishes make small pies for each person. Just cook them slightly less, about 20 minutes.

214

SERVES 4

Chicken with Mashed Potatoes

PREPARATION TIME 15 MINUTES

COOKING TIME 30 MINUTES

INGREDIENTS

4 chicken breasts, skinned
2 bunches fresh basil leaves
salt and pepper
1.5 kg / 3 lb / 6 ⅓ cups floury potatoes, peeled and cubed
100 g / 3 ½ oz / ½ cup butter
100 ml / 3 ½ fl. oz / ½ cup milk
2 tomatoes, skinned, deseeded and finely chopped
1 tbsp capers
olive oil

- Wrap the chicken breasts carefully in basil leaves, seasoning each chicken breast before wrapping.
- Steam the chicken over simmering water until cooked through and the juices run clear—about 20 minutes.
- Meanwhile cook the potatoes in boiling salted water until tender. Drain thoroughly and return to the heat briefly to dry out.
- Mash well with the butter and milk until completely smooth. Season well. Gently toss together the tomatoes, capers and a little oil.
- Serve the chicken with a spoon of mashed potato alongside, scattered with the tomato mixture.

Chicken with Ham and Basil 215

- Try wrapping the chicken in basil then in cured ham for a stronger flavour.

216

SERVES 4

Chicken Liver Tagliatelle with Blue Cheese

- Heat the butter in a pan and when foaming add the livers. Sauté until golden and just blushing pink inside, then remove from the pan with a slotted spoon.
- Add the peppers and sauté over high heat until tender, then pour in the cream and add the cheese, stirring until smooth. Adjust the seasoning if necessary.
- Meanwhile cook the tagliatelle according to packet instructions, then drain, reserving a cupful of the cooking water.
- Add a little of the water to the sauce to loosen then toss with the tagliatelle.
- Serve on warm plates topped with the chicken livers and grated Parmesan.

PREPARATION TIME 10 MINUTES

COOKING TIME 20 MINUTES

INGREDIENTS

40 g / 1 oz butter
200 g / 7 oz / ¾ cup chicken livers, trimmed and chopped
2 red peppers, deseeded and sliced
200 ml / 7 fl. oz / ¾ cup double (heavy) cream
75 g / 2 ½ oz / ⅓ cup blue cheese, crumbled
salt and pepper
350 g / 12 oz / 1 ⅓ cups tagliatelle
Parmesan, grated

Chicken Liver Tagliatelle with Cream

217

- If the blue cheese is too strong, just miss it out and add a splash of Vermouth to the peppers before the cream.

218

SERVES 4

Griddled Chicken with Farfalle

- Cook the pasta in boiling salted water according to packet instructions. Drain, reserving a little of the water.
- Meanwhile heat the oil in a pan and fry or griddle the chicken until golden and cooked through. Season.
- Toss the pasta with the extra virgin olive oil and lemon juice, adding a little cooking water to lubricate and season.
- Serve hot tossed with the cherry tomatoes, spring onions, spinach and Parmesan and the chicken arranged on top.

PREPARATION TIME 5 MINUTES

COOKING TIME 15 MINUTES

INGREDIENTS

2 chicken breasts, thinly sliced
2 tbsp olive oil
salt and pepper
500 g / 1 lb / 2 cups farfalle pasta
2 tbsp extra virgin olive oil
1 tbsp lemon juice
16 cherry tomatoes, halved
4 spring onions (scallions), thinly sliced
2 large handfuls baby spinach leaves
25 g / 1 oz / ¼ cup Parmesan, shaved

Griddled Chicken with Farfalle and Artichokes

 219

- Try adding bottled artichokes to the pasta instead of the spinach.

220

SERVES 4–6

Roast Chicken with Orange and Fennel

PREPARATION TIME 10 MINUTES

COOKING TIME
1 HOUR 30 MINUTES

INGREDIENTS

1 oven ready chicken
1 tbsp fennel seeds, lightly crushed
4 tbsp olive oil
1 orange, zested
salt and pepper
1 orange
4 carrots, peeled and cut into short lengths
1 onion, quartered
4 sprigs thyme

- Preheat the oven to 220°C (200°C fan) / 425F / gas 7.
- Mix together the fennel seeds, half the oil, the zest and seasoning and rub over the skin of the chicken. Place the chicken in a roasting tin. Roast in the oven for 20 minutes.
- Reduce the heat to 180°C (160°C fan) / 350F / gas 4.
- Cut the orange into thick slices. Tip into the roasting tin around the chicken with the carrots and onion and toss with the remaining oil, tucking the thyme sprigs around. Season and cook for 1 hour or until the juices run clear when pierced with a toothpick.
- Leave the chicken to rest for 20 minutes before carving and serving with the vegetables.

Roast Chicken with Coriander and Orange

221

- Coriander (cilantro) seeds have a citrus hint and work well with the orange.

222

SERVES 2

Pan-fried Chicory, Chicken and Peanuts

PREPARATION TIME 10 MINUTES

COOKING TIME 10 MINUTES

INGREDIENTS

2 tbsp olive oil
2 chicken thighs, skinned, deboned and chopped
2 heads of chicory, separated into leaves and chopped
½ orange, juiced
2 tomatoes, cored and diced
2 tbsp peanuts, crushed
salt and pepper

- Heat the oil in a pan and briskly fry the chicken until golden and cooked through.
- Add the chicory and cook until wilted, then stir in the orange juice and tomatoes.
- Spoon onto plates and sprinkle over peanuts and seasoning, then serve.

Pan-fried Chicory

223

- Halve the chicory and core, then fry cut side down gently in butter and white wine with a lid on until tender.

224

SERVES 4

Chicken with Potatoes and Pumpkin

Chicken With
Sautéed Fennel

225

- Try using a thickly sliced fennel bulb in place of the pumpkin for a cleaner flavour.

Chicken with
Sauteed Turnips

226

- Sweet baby turnips would be perfect in early spring.

PREPARATION TIME 15 MINUTES

COOKING TIME 30 MINUTES

INGREDIENTS

4 chicken supremes, bone-in, skin on
3 tbsp olive oil
salt and pepper
30 g / 1 oz butter
1 kg / 2 lb / 4 ¼ cups new potatoes, scrubbed
1 small pumpkin or butternut squash, peeled, deseeded and cubed
2 sprigs thyme
100 ml / 3 ½ fl. oz / ½ cup chicken stock

- Preheat the oven to 200°C (180°C fan) / 400F / gas 6.
- Drizzle the chicken with oil, season and roast in the oven for 25 minutes or until just cooked.
- Meanwhile, heat the butter in a pan and sauté the potatoes and pumpkin, adding the chicken stock once they are golden in patches. Add the thyme, season and leave to cook until tender – about 15 minutes.
- Slice the chicken thickly and serve with the sautéed potatoes and pumpkin.

227

SERVES 4

Chicken with Stuffed Roasted Peppers

Cheesy Stuffed Peppers

228

- Add a chunk of mozzarella or bocconcini to each pepper for the last 10 minutes.

Chicken with Roasted Vegetables

229

- If time is short, simply roast cubed aubergine and peppers instead.

PREPARATION TIME 15 MINUTES

COOKING TIME 40 MINUTES

INGREDIENTS

4 red peppers, halved and deseeded
8 cherry tomatoes
8 anchovy fillets
150 ml / 5 fl. oz / ⅔ cup extra virgin olive oil
4 chicken breasts, skin on
salt and pepper
150 ml / 5 fl. oz / ⅔ cup passata
1 clove of garlic, crushed
chopped fresh parsley

- Preheat the oven to 220°C (200°C fan) / 425F / gas 7.
- Sit the halved peppers in a roasting tin, then fill the cavities with tomatoes, tucking the anchovies underneath them and adding a good drizzle of extra virgin olive oil. Roast in the oven for 30–40 minutes until the peppers are tender and collapsing.
- Meanwhile roast the chicken alongside, drizzled with oil and seasoned for the last 20 minutes.
- Heat the passata in a small pan with the garlic and season.
- Serve the halved roasted peppers on a plate, slice the chicken and arrange on top then spoon the sauce around and scatter with parsley.

230
SERVES 4–6

Chicken with Vanilla and Carrot Mash

- Preheat the oven to 200°C (180°C fan) / 400F / gas 6.
- Drizzle the chicken with oil, season and pour the wine into the bottom of the roasting tin. Roast in the oven for about 30 minutes or until the chicken is cooked through, covering with foil if it looks too brown.
- Meanwhile, cook the carrots in the vegetable stock until tender. You may need to add more water if it looks too dry. Drain, reserving the cooking liquid and mash with butter. Season well and keep hot.
- When the chicken is cooked, remove to a serving platter and place the roasting tin over the heat. Split the vanilla pods in half, scrape out the seeds and add with the pods to the tin. Add the bay leaves and a little carrot cooking liquid and deglaze to make a sauce. Simmer until reduced, season and add a little lemon juice.
- Serve with chicken with the carrot mash and spoon over the sauce.

Chicken with Mixed Vegetable Mash
231

- Sweet root vegetables go well with the vanilla, so use swede or parsnip for a change.

PREPARATION TIME 10 MINUTES

COOKING TIME 30–40 MINUTES

INGREDIENTS

1 chicken, jointed
4 tbsp olive oil
200 ml / 7 fl. oz / ¾ cup white wine
salt and pepper
1 kg / 2 lb / 4 ¼ cups carrots, peeled and chopped
300 ml / 10 fl. oz / 1 ¼ cups vegetable stock
30 g / 1 oz butter
3 vanilla pods
2 bay leaves
½ lemon, juiced

232
SERVES 4

Chicken, Courgette and Walnut Crumble

- Poach the chicken in the stock for 5 minutes until just cooked through. Drain, reserving the stock.
- Heat the butter in a pan and sauté the onion and courgette until golden, then add the chicken. Add the cream and basil and enough poaching liquor to loosen a little, then season and set aside.
- Meanwhile rub the butter and flour together with your fingertips to resemble breadcrumbs, then stir through the walnuts and season well.
- Spoon the chicken mixture into a gratin dish, then top lightly with the crumble. Grill or bake until bubbling and the topping is golden and crunchy.

Chicken Crumble with Hazelnuts and Pumpkin
233

- Autumnal hazelnuts (cob nuts) complement the sweetness of pumpkin.

PREPARATION TIME 20 MINUTES

COOKING TIME 10–20 MINUTES

INGREDIENTS

4 chicken breasts, skinned and cubed
500 ml / 1 pint / 2 cups chicken stock
40 g / 1 oz butter
1 onion, peeled and chopped
2 courgettes (zucchini), thinly sliced lengthways
200 ml / 7 fl. oz / ¾ cup double (heavy) cream
½ bunch basil leaves
salt and pepper

FOR THE CRUMBLE
120 g / 4 oz / ½ cup plain (all purpose) flour
100 g / 3 ½ oz / ½ cup butter, cold and cubed
50 g / 1 ¾ oz / ¼ cup walnuts, chopped

234

SERVES 4

Sesame Seed Chicken

PREPARATION TIME 10 MINUTES

COOKING TIME 15 MINUTES

INGREDIENTS

4 chicken pieces, bone in
4 tbsp olive oil
2 cloves of garlic, crushed
½ bunch parsley, finely chopped
1 tbsp Dijon mustard
salt and pepper
4 tbsp sesame seeds
½ lemon, juiced

- Whisk together the oil, garlic, parsley, mustard and some seasoning and coat the chicken pieces thoroughly in the marinade.
- Heat a deep sided pan with a little oil and cook the chicken in batches until golden and cooked through - about 15 minutes.
- Coat in the sesame seeds, squeeze over a little lemon juice and serve hot or cold.

235

SERVES 4

Chicken with Prawns and Spaghetti

PREPARATION TIME 5 MINUTES

COOKING TIME 30 MINUTES

INGREDIENTS

4 chicken thighs
4 tbsp olive oil
1 tsp oregano or rosemary leaves, chopped
salt and pepper
320 g / 11 oz / 1 ⅓ cups spaghetti
225 g / 8 oz / 1 cup raw king prawns
1 onion, peeled and finely chopped
pinch dried chilli (chili) flakes
1 clove of garlic, crushed

- Preheat the oven to 200°C (180°C fan) / 400F / gas 6.
- Drizzle the chicken thighs with half the oil, sprinkle with herbs and seasoning and roast in the oven for 25 minutes or until golden and cooked through.
- Meanwhile cook the pasta in boiling salted water according to packet instructions. Drain, reserving a little of the pasta cooking water.
- While the chicken is resting, heat the remaining oil in a pan with the onion, chilli and garlic and cook until softened. Add the prawns. Toss and cook for a few minutes until pink, then add the spaghetti and any roasting juices from the chicken. Toss to coat, then add a splash of pasta cooking water to emulsify the sauce.
- Serve the pasta and prawns in deep warmed bowls, topped with chicken.

SERVES 4–6

Chicken with Courgette and Olives

- Preheat the oven to 200°C (180°C fan) / 400F / gas 6.
- Marinate the chicken in the lemon zest, juice, oregano, garlic and half the oil for 30 minutes.
- Tip the chicken into a large roasting tin and add the onions, courgettes, remaining oil, white wine and season well. Roast for 30 minutes, or until just cooked through.
- Add the olives for the last 5 minutes of cooking, so they don't harden in the heat of the oven.
- Serve with all the pan juices.

PREPARATION TIME 40 MINUTES

COOKING TIME 30–35 MINUTES

INGREDIENTS

4 chicken portions, boned and cut into large pieces
zest and juice of ½ lemon
1 tbsp dried oregano
2 cloves of garlic, crushed
7 tbsp olive oil
4 small red onions, peeled and quartered
4 courgettes (zucchini), chunks
splash white wine
salt and pepper
50 g / 1 ¾ oz / ¼ cup mixed olives

Mediterranean Chicken

237
SERVES 4–6

PREPARATION TIME 40 MINUTES

COOKING TIME 30–35 MINUTES

INGREDIENTS

1 chicken, jointed into 6 pieces
½ lemon, juiced and zested
1 tbsp dried oregano
2 cloves of garlic, crushed

6 tbsp olive oil
2 red peppers, deseeded and roughly chopped
2 yellow peppers, deseeded and roughly chopped
splash white wine
salt and pepper
50 g / 1 ¾ oz / ¼ cup black olives
flat leaf parsley sprigs

- Preheat the oven to 200°C (180°C fan) / 400F / gas 6.
- Marinate the chicken in the lemon zest, juice, oregano, garlic and half the oil for 30 minutes.
- Tip the chicken into a large roasting tin and add the peppers, remaining oil, white wine and season well. Roast for 30 minutes, or until just cooked through.
- Add the olives for the last 5 minutes of cooking, so they don't harden in the heat of the oven.
- Serve with all the pan juices and parsley sprigs scattered over.

Vanilla Chicken with Figs

238
SERVES 4

PREPARATION TIME 20 MINUTES

COOKING TIME 20 MINUTES

INGREDIENTS

4 chicken breasts
100 ml / 3 ½ fl. oz / ½ cup cider or white wine vinegar
100 ml / 3 ½ fl. oz / ½ cup rum

100 g / 3 ½ oz / ½ cup soft brown sugar
1 vanilla pod
salt and pepper
250 g / 9 oz / 1 cup couscous
250 ml / 9 fl. oz / 1 cup chicken or vegetable stock
squeeze of lemon juice
8 figs, quartered

- Mix together the vinegar, rum and sugar. Split the vanilla pod in half down the middle and scrape out the seeds. Add to the marinade with seasoning. Simmer in a small pan for 5 minutes until the sugar has dissolved. Leave to cool.
- Coat the chicken in the marinade and refrigerate for at least 1 hour.
- Preheat the oven to 190°C (170°C fan) / 375F / gas 5.
- Sit the chicken in a foil-lined roasting tin and roast for 20–25 minutes until cooked through and golden. Reserve any remaining marinade.
- Tip the reserved marinade into a small pan and simmer gently for 5 minutes.
- Tip the couscous into a bowl, cover with the hot stock and cover over with cling film. Leave for 10 minutes or so until tender, then fork through and season and add lemon juice.
- Serve the chicken with the sauce drizzled over, the figs and couscous alongside.

239

SERVES 6

Chicken Stuffed with Mushrooms

Chestnut, Bacon and Mushroom Stuffing

240

- Add 2 rashers finely chopped smoked streaky bacon for oomph and a smoked taste.

Chicken Stuffed with Sage and Portobellos

241

- Swap the tarragon for ½ a bunch of sage and use Portobello mushrooms instead of ceps for a subtle flavour.

PREPARATION TIME 20 MINUTES

COOKING TIME
1 HOUR 30 MINUTES

....

INGREDIENTS

1 oven ready chicken
1.5 kg / 3 lb / 6 cups potatoes, peeled and cut into chunks
150 ml / 5 fl. oz / ⅔ cup milk
100 g / 3 ½ oz / ½ cup butter
3 eggs, beaten
salt and pepper

FOR THE STUFFING
2 tbsp butter
500 g / 1 lb / 2 cups cep or other wild mushrooms, chopped
1 onion, finely chopped
1 clove of garlic, chopped
10 vacuum packed chestnuts, chopped
½ bunch tarragon
1 slice bread, soaked in milk
1 egg, beaten

- Preheat the oven to 220°C (200°C fan) / 425F / gas 7.
- Heat the butter in a pan and cook the mushrooms, onion and garlic until tender. Leave to cool. Mix with the chestnuts, tarragon, crumbled bread and egg, then stuff into the cavity of the chicken.
- Season the chicken all over, drizzle with oil and roast in the oven for 20 minutes.
- Reduce the heat to 180°C (160°C fan) / 350F / gas 4 and roast for 1 hour until cooked through.
- Meanwhile cook the potatoes in boiling salted water until tender to the point of a knife. Drain thoroughly and return briefly to the heat to drive off any excess water. Mash the potatoes thoroughly with a potato ricer or hand-held masher.
- Heat the milk and butter until the butter has melted, then stir into the potatoes with 2 of the beaten eggs and season well.
- Spoon into a piping bag with a 1.25 cm (½ in) star nozzle and pipe into swirls onto a greased baking tray. Brush with the remaining egg.
- When the chicken has cooked turn the oven back up to 220°C (200°C fan) / 425F / gas 7 and bake the potatoes for 15 minutes or until golden while the chicken is resting.

242

SERVES 4

Pan-fried Chicken with Vegetables

- Heat the oil in a pan and fry the chicken on both sides until golden.
- Tip the vegetables and garlic into the pan and sauté to lightly colour, then add the wine, sage and thyme, put the lid on and leave to simmer for 10–15 minutes until all is cooked.
- Season and serve.

PREPARATION TIME 10 MINUTES

COOKING TIME 30 MINUTES

....

INGREDIENTS

2 tbsp olive oil
4 chicken legs
4 carrots, peeled and cut
into short lengths
2 leeks, trimmed and thickly sliced
4 whole garlic cloves, peeled
150 ml / 5 fl. oz / ⅔ cup dry
white wine
few sprigs sage leaves
pinch of thyme leaves
salt and pepper

Pan-fried Chicken with Fennel and Potatoes

243

- Try substituting the leeks and carrots with quartered fennel, new potatoes and a tsp of fennel seeds.

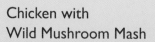

244

SERVES 4

Chicken with Wild Mushrooms

- Preheat the oven to 180°C (160°C fan) / 350F / gas 4.
- Mix together the honey, mustard, oil and seasoning and roll the chicken in the mixture to coat thoroughly. Place in a foil-lined roasting tin and roast in the oven, turning once, for 30 minutes until sticky and cooked through.
- Meanwhile heat the butter in a pan and sweat the shallot rings and garlic without colouring. Add the mushrooms and sauté briskly until the liquid has evaporated. Season.
- Serve the drumsticks with the mushrooms and shallots spooned around.

PREPARATION TIME 10 MINUTES

COOKING TIME 30 MINUTES

....

INGREDIENTS

4 chicken drumsticks
2 tbsp runny honey
1 ½ tbsp grain mustard
1 tbsp olive oil
salt and pepper
40 g / 1 oz butter
2 shallots, finely sliced into rings
2 cloves of garlic, chopped
250 g / 9 oz / 1 cup wild mushrooms,
cleaned

Chicken with Wild Mushroom Mash

245

- To make a substantial side dish, try folding the mushroom mix into creamy mashed potato.

Lemon and Chervil Chicken

PREPARATION TIME 5 MINUTES

COOKING TIME 15–20 MINUTES

INGREDIENTS

2 tbsp butter
2 chicken breasts, skin on
1 lemon
½ bunch chervil, chopped
200 ml / 7 fl. oz / ¾ cup white wine
250 g / 9 oz / 1 cup green beans, trimmed
salt and pepper

- Heat the butter in a pan and cook the chicken gently skin side down until golden and crisp.
- Turn over and cook on the other side for 5 minutes.
- Meanwhile remove the zest from the lemon and finely shred.
- When the chicken is cooked, remove to a plate to rest and deglaze the pan with the white wine. Add the zest and chervil, season and reduce until syrupy. Adjust the acidity with a little lemon juice.
- Meanwhile steam the green beans for 4 minutes over simmering water.
- Serve the chicken with the sauce and green beans.

Orange Chicken Escalopes 247

- Substitute the lemon for orange for a different citrus burst.

248
SERVES 4

Chicken Aubergine Colombo

PREPARATION TIME 15 MINUTES

COOKING TIME 30 MINUTES

INGREDIENTS

1 tbsp vegetable oil
4 chicken thighs, skinned, deboned and cubed
salt and pepper
1 onion, peeled and sliced
1 aubergine (eggplant), diced
3 cloves of garlic, crushed
2 tbsp curry powder
6 sprigs thyme leaves
1 tsp ground allspice
½ tsp ground cinnamon
2 bay leaves
1–2 Scotch Bonnet chillies (chilies)
500 ml / 1 pint / 2 cups chicken stock
400 g / 14 oz / 1 ½ cups chopped tomatoes
1 lime, quartered

- Heat the oil and sear the chicken on all sides until golden. Remove with a slotted spoon and set aside.
- Add the onion and aubergines and cook until softened, then add the garlic, herbs and spices and cook for 2 minutes.
- Add the chillies, stock and tomatoes and bring to a simmer. Add the chicken back to the pan, reduce the heat, cover with a lid and cook for 20 minutes until the chicken is cooked.
- Remove the chillies, adjust the seasoning and serve with the quartered limes.

Chicken and Sweet Potato Colombo 249

- Add diced sweet potatoes to make this more substantial.

250

SERVES 4

Chicken and Leek Parcels

- Preheat the oven to 200°C (180°C fan) / 400F / gas 6.
- Lay out 4 pieces of greaseproof paper and place a chicken breast in the centre of each one.
- Top with the leeks, tomatoes, some lemon zest and juice, a splash of white wine and a tarragon sprig. Season.
- Fold the paper into parcels, scrunching to seal and bake in the oven on a baking sheet for about 25 minutes.
- Serve at the table for everyone to open their own parcels.

PREPARATION TIME 10 MINUTES

COOKING TIME 25 MINUTES

···

INGREDIENTS

4 chicken breasts, skinned
1 leek, trimmed and sliced lengthways
4 tomatoes, thickly sliced
1 lemon, juiced and zested
4 sprigs tarragon
100 ml / 3 ½ fl. oz / ½ cup white wine
salt and pepper

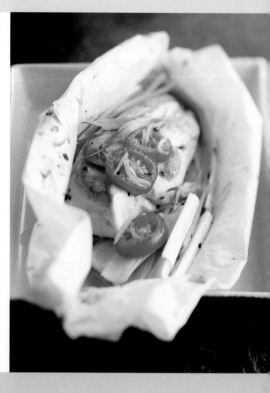

Fragrant Chicken Parcels

 251

- Try adding a little lemongrass, lime or curry leaves and fennel seeds for a curried version.

 252

SERVES 4

Cider Chicken with Apples

- Preheat the oven to 220°C (200°C fan) / 425F / gas 7.
- Place the chicken in a roasting tin and smear with the butter. Season well and push the thyme sprigs into the cavity. Place in the oven and roast for 20 minutes.
- Turn the heat down to 180°C (160°C fan) / 350F / gas 4.
- Add the potatoes to the pan and roast the chicken for another 30 minutes.
- Pour 200 ml of cider into the pan, add the apples and onions and roast for another 30–40 minutes.
- Remove the chicken, potatoes and apples to a serving platter to rest, loosely covered with foil, then place the roasting tin back on the hob. Add enough cider to make a sauce, scraping at the base of the pan with a wooden spoon and simmer until reduced to your liking. Season.
- Serve the chicken with the apples and potatoes, the sauce poured over.

PREPARATION TIME 10 MINUTES

COOKING TIME
1 HOUR 45 MINUTES

···

INGREDIENTS

1 oven ready chicken
30 g / 1 oz butter, softened
salt and pepper
4 sprigs thyme
500 ml / 1 pint / 2 cups dry cider
2 crisp eating apples, sliced into wedges
1 kg / 2 lb / 4 cups waxy potatoes, cut into wedges
1 bunch spring onions (scallions), halved

Creamy Cider Chicken

253

- 2 tbsp creme fraîche added to the sauce once reduced makes for a creamier indulgent sauce.

254

SERVES 4

Basque Chicken with Bacon

Meaty Basque Chicken   255

- Add chopped chorizo or even spicy sausages cut into chunks for extra protein punch.

Sweet Potato Wedges   256

- Roast wedges of unpeeled sweet potato with oil and seasoning for 30 minutes to serve alongside.

PREPARATION TIME 10 MINUTES

COOKING TIME 40 MINUTES

INGREDIENTS

2 tbsp olive oil
4 chicken legs
1 onion, chopped
2 cloves of garlic, chopped
150 g / 5 oz / ⅔ cup pancetta or smoked streaky bacon, chopped
1 red pepper, deseeded and sliced
1 green pepper, deseeded and sliced
1 yellow pepper, deseeded and sliced
6 ripe vine tomatoes, cored and chopped
2 bay leaves
1 tsp sugar
1 tsp smoked paprika
salt and pepper

- Heat the oil in a pan and brown the legs until golden. Remove to a plate and set aside.
- Add the onion and garlic with the pancetta and cook gently until golden, then add the chicken back to the pan along with the peppers and tomatoes, bay leaves, sugar, paprika and seasoning and allow to simmer for about 20–25 minutes until all is cooked. Adjust the seasoning to taste.

273

SERVES 4

Chinese Chicken Stir-fry

Chinese Chicken Baguettes

274

- Spoon the hot stir-fry into hot baguettes.

Chicken Squid Stir-fry

275

- Add frozen defrosted squid rings to the stir-fry for texture.

PREPARATION TIME 10 MINUTES

COOKING TIME 10–12 MINUTES

INGREDIENTS

2 tbsp vegetable oil
350 g / 12 oz / 1 ½ cups chicken thigh meat, diced
1 red onion, peeled and finely sliced
2 cloves of garlic, finely sliced
1 tsp fresh ginger, grated
1 red and 1 green pepper, deseeded and finely sliced
½ bunch spring onions (scallions), sliced
200 g / 7 oz / ¾ cup baby sweetcorn, sliced
100 g / 3 ½ oz / ½ cup shiitake mushrooms, sliced
75–100 ml / 2 ½–3 ½ fl. oz / ⅓–½ cup soy sauce
2 tbsp rice wine (mirin)
2-3 tbsp sweet chilli (chili) sauce
salt and pepper

- Heat the oil in a wok until nearly smoking, then add the chicken. Stir-fry over a high heat until golden all over and the fat crisp. Remove from the pan with a slotted spoon.
- Add the onion, garlic and ginger and stir-fry for 2 minutes. Add the vegetables and cook until crisp-tender. Add the meat back to the pan and stir in the sauces and wine.
- Leave to bubble for a few minutes then check and adjust the seasoning if necessary.

276

SERVES 8

Chicken and Tarragon Cake

PREPARATION TIME 20 MINUTES

COOKING TIME 40 MINUTES

INGREDIENTS

3 eggs
½ tsp sugar
235 g / 8 oz / 1 cup plain
(all purpose) flour
60 g / 2 oz / ¼ cup potato flour
2 tsp baking powder
½ tsp salt
6 tbsp olive oil
2 tbsp sour cream
2 chicken breasts, cooked and
finely chopped
280 g / 9 ½ oz / 1 ¼ cups
sun-dried tomatoes, chopped
1 tbsp tarragon leaves, finely
chopped
2 handfuls mache (corn salad)
2 handfuls rocket (arugula)
2 tbsp Parmesan shavings

- Preheat oven to 190°C (170°C fan) / 375F / gas 5.
- Whisk the eggs and sugar together until pale and thick.
- Sieve the flours, baking powder and salt into a bowl, then fold into the eggs. Stir in the sour cream and oil until incorporated. Stir in the tomatoes, chicken and tarragon leaves.
- Grease and line a 900 g / 1 lb loaf tin, then pour in the mixture, bake in the oven for about 40 minutes until a skewer inserted into the middle comes out clean.
- Remove to a wire rack and allow to cool.
- Toss together the salad leaves and Parmesan and serve with the chicken loaf cake.

277

SERVES 4

Chicken, Pepper and Bacon Tagine

PREPARATION TIME 20 MINUTES

COOKING TIME 45 MINUTES

INGREDIENTS

2 tbsp olive oil
1 onion, peeled and thickly sliced
2 cloves of garlic, finely sliced
4 rashers streaky bacon, diced
4 chicken legs
2 yellow peppers, deseeded and
chopped
1 tsp curry powder
1 tsp ground coriander (cilantro) seeds
1 tsp ground cumin
4 preserved lemons, chopped
400 g / 14 oz / 1 ½ cups canned
tomatoes
200 ml / 7 fl. oz / ¾ cup chicken stock
2 tbsp green olives
½ bunch coriander (cilantro), chopped
salt and pepper

- Heat the oil in a large pan and cook the onions until golden and tender.
- Add the bacon and garlic and cook for a few minutes, then remove all from the pan with a slotted spoon. Add the peppers and cook for a few minutes.
- Increase the heat and brown the chicken on all sides, then tip the onion mixture back into the pan and sprinkle over the spices and preserved lemons.
- Pour over the canned tomatoes and stock and season, lower the heat and cook gently for about 45 minutes or until the sauce has thickened and the chicken is cooked.
- Add the olives to warm through, adjust the seasoning and sprinkle with coriander.

278

SERVES 4

Crispy Chicken with Sweet Potato Mash

- Cube the chicken and place in a bowl with the buttermilk. Refrigerate for at least 2 hours or even overnight.
- Cut the potatoes into large chunks and cook in boiling salted water until tender – about 10–12 minutes. Drain thoroughly, then set the pan over a low heat and shake the pan to drive off any excess moisture.
- Mash with the butter until fairly smooth then season generously, stir through the herbs and keep warm.
- Dip the chicken cubes one at a time into the flour, egg then breadcrumbs and lay on a rack to dry slightly.
- Heat 1 cm (½ in) depth oil in a pan and fry the chicken in batches until golden on both sides and cooked through.
- Serve the chicken with the warm mash, and chopped coriander to garnish.

PREPARATION TIME 15 MINUTES
+ MARINATING TIME

COOKING TIME 20 MINUTES

....

INGREDIENTS

4 chicken breasts, skinned
300 ml / 10 fl.oz / 1 ¼ cups buttermilk
100 g / 3 ½ oz / ½ cup plain
(all purpose) flour
2 eggs, beaten
200 g / 7 oz / ¾ cup breadcrumbs,
vegetable oil
4 large sweet potatoes, peeled
salt and pepper
50 g / 1 ¾ oz / ¼ cup butter
1 tbsp chopped coriander (cilantro)

279

SERVES 4

Chicken Pasanda

PREPARATION TIME 15 MINUTES

COOKING TIME
1 HOUR 15 MINUTES

....

INGREDIENTS

2 tbsp vegetable oil
1 onion, peeled and finely chopped
1 cinnamon stick
2 cardamom pods, lightly crushed

3 cm / 1 inch piece ginger
2 cloves of garlic, finely sliced
1 tsp turmeric, 1 tsp ground cumin
1 tsp ground coriander, 1 tsp paprika
½–1 tsp chilli (chili) powder
150 ml / 5 fl. oz / ⅔ cup plain
yoghurt
2 tbsp tomato puree
2 chicken breasts, skinned
4 tbsp flaked (slivered) almonds
rice to serve

- Heat the oil in a pan and fry the onion until golden. Add the cinnamon and cardamom, ginger and garlic and cook gently for another 5–10 minutes until soft.
- Add the turmeric, cumin, coriander, paprika and chilli and fry for 1 minute, then add 1 tbsp yoghurt and cook so it sizzles and starts to dry out – don't worry if it splits or looks odd.
- Repeat until all the yoghurt is incorporated then add the tomato puree and around 250 ml / 9 fl oz / 1 cup hot water and simmer for 20–30 minutes.
- Chop the chicken.
- Toast the almonds in a dry frying pan, then crush and stir into the sauce with the chicken and simmer for 20 minutes. Add more water if the sauce looks too dry. Adjust the seasoning.
- Remove the cinnamon stick and cardamom and serve with the rice.

280

SERVES 4

Mediterranean Tray-bake

PREPARATION TIME 10 MINUTES

COOKING TIME 30–40 MINUTES

....

INGREDIENTS

4 chicken breasts, skin on
2 courgettes (zucchini), thickly sliced
2 red peppers, deseeded and roughly chopped

2 orange peppers, deseeded and roughly chopped
2 red onions, peeled and cut into eighths
400 g / 14 oz / 1 ½ cups canned tomatoes
2 tbsp olive oil
2 tbsp dried Herbes de Provence
salt and pepper
100 g / 3 ½ oz / ½ cup green olives

- Preheat the oven to 180°C (160°C fan) / 350F / gas 4.
- Place the chicken and vegetables in a roasting tin, pour over the tomatoes, sprinkle over herbs, oil and seasoning and roast for 30–40 minutes until the chicken is cooked.
- Add the olives for the last 5 minutes of cooking.
- Serve at the table for everyone to help themselves.

281

SERVES 4

Stuffed Chicken with Monkfish Bites

PREPARATION TIME 45 MINUTES

COOKING TIME 45–50 MINUTES

INGREDIENTS

100 g / 3 ½ oz / ½ cup dried figs
200 ml / 7 fl. oz / ¾ cup marsala
6 tbsp olive oil
1 onion, peeled and finely diced
2 rashers streaky bacon, diced
100 g / 3 ½ oz / ½ cup pistachios, chopped, plus extra to serve
1 tbsp parsley, chopped
½ orange, zested
350 g / 12 oz / 1 ¼ cups breadcrumbs
salt and pepper
4 chicken legs, deboned, skin on
8 dates
400 g / 14 oz / 1 ½ cups monkfish tail, boned
3 tbsp flour
2 eggs, beaten
1 tsp dried thyme
75 ml / 2 ½ fl. oz / ⅓ cup rice

- Preheat the oven to 180°C (160°C fan) / 350F / gas 4.
- Halve the figs, then soak in the marsala for 20 minutes.
- Fry the onion, bacon and pistachios in 2 tbsp oil until golden, then add the parsley and orange zest.
- Lift the figs from the alcohol, reserving the liquid, and finely chop, then add to the stuffing mix with half the breadcrumbs and mix well.
- Lay chicken legs skin-side down and divide the stuffing between them. Truss with cook's string, to make round parcels. Place in a tin and roast for 45 minutes.
- Meanwhile cut the monkfish into chunks, coat in flour, egg and rest of breadcrumbs mixed with thyme, then shallow fry in the remaining oil until golden.
- Pour the reserved marsala into a pan, add the dates and reduce. Serve the chicken parcels with the monkfish bites and extra pistachios.

Chicken Parcels with Pistachio Couscous

282

- Stir chopped pistachios into steamed couscous for a change from rice.

283

SERVES 4

Caramelised Chicken, Griddled Corn and Rice

PREPARATION TIME 15 MINUTES

COOKING TIME 30 MINUTES

INGREDIENTS

8 chicken drumsticks
olive oil
salt and pepper
4 sweetcorn, peeled
100 g / 3 ½ oz / ½ cup green beans, trimmed
rice to serve

FOR THE BARBECUE SAUCE
4 tbsp white wine vinegar
3–4 tbsp soy sauce
2–3 tbsp tomato ketchup
1 tbsp soft brown sugar
2 tsp English mustard powder
1 tsp paprika
pinch dried chilli (chili) flakes
salt and pepper

- Preheat the oven to 200°C (180°C fan) / 400F / gas 6.
- Mix together the sauce ingredients and simmer in a pan for 5 minutes, then coat the drumsticks thoroughly in the sauce.
- Lay the drumsticks in a foil-lined roasting tin and roast in the oven for about 25 minutes until golden and cooked through. If they look like they are burning, cover with foil.
- Meanwhile heat a griddle or barbecue until smoking and cook the sweetcorn, turning frequently until lightly charred and tender.
- Steam the green beans over simmering water for 4–5 minutes until crisp-tender.
- Serve the hot chicken with the rice, corn and beans and any sauce spooned over.

Chicken, Corn and Vegetable Rice

284

- Add cooked peas and drained canned black-eye beans to the rice.

285

SERVES 4

Breaded Chicken Breast with Salad

- Place the chicken between 2 pieces of cling film and bash out a little with a rolling pin to about 2 cm (1 in) thickness. Cut each breast into 2 pieces.
- Place the chicken in a bowl with the buttermilk. Refrigerate for at least 2 hours or even overnight.
- Dip the chicken breasts one at a time into the flour, egg then breadcrumbs mixed with mustard powder and lay on a rack to dry slightly.
- Heat 1cm depth oil in a pan and fry the chicken in batches until golden on both sides and cooked through.
- Serve with salad and lemon wedges.

PREPARATION TIME 10 MINUTES

COOKING TIME 15–20 MINUTES

INGREDIENTS

4 chicken breasts, skinned
300 ml / 10 fl. oz / 1 ¼ cups buttermilk
100 g / 3 ½ oz / ½ cup plain (all purpose) flour
2 eggs, beaten
200 g / 7 oz / ¾ cup breadcrumbs
1 tsp mustard powder
vegetable oil
mixed salad, to serve
lemon wedges, to serve

Crispy Chicken Muffins

286

- Toast English muffins and top with mayonnaise, tomatoes and crisp chicken cut into slices.

287

SERVES 4

Chicken with Apple Sauce

- Preheat the oven to 200°C (180°C fan) / 400F / gas 6.
- Cook the rice according to packet instructions, drain and keep warm.
- Meanwhile drizzle the chicken with oil, season well and roast in the oven for 25 minutes.
- Peel and core the apples and cut into chunks. Place in a pan with the sugar, cloves, vinegar and water and cover with a lid.
- Cook over a low heat for 10–15 minutes, checking occasionally, until the apples are soft. Beat until fairly smooth and remove the cloves.
- Cook the Brussels tops briefly in boiling salted water then drain thoroughly.
- Serve the chicken with the apple sauce, rice and Brussel tops.

PREPARATION TIME 15 MINUTES

COOKING TIME 35 MINUTES

INGREDIENTS

4 chicken supremes, skin on
2 tbsp olive oil
salt and pepper
250 g / 9 oz / 1 cup Bramley apples
250 g / 9 oz / 1 cup Cox apples
1 tbsp sugar (optional, depending on tartness of apples)
2 cloves
2 tbsp water
1 tbsp cider vinegar
250 g / 9 oz / 1 cup Brussels sprout tops
250 g / 9 oz / 1 cup white and wild rice

Chicken with Carrots and Apple Sauce

288

- Replace the brussels with carrots.

296

SERVES 4

Roast Chicken with Figs and Rösti

Roast Chicken with Pears and Rösti

297

- Replace the figs with pear slices.

Apple Potato Rösti

298

- Add 1 grated eating apple to the mix for a slightly sweet twist.

PREPARATION TIME 20 MINUTES

COOKING TIME 30–35 MINUTES

....

INGREDIENTS

4 chicken supremes, skin on
2 tbsp olive oil
salt and pepper
2 tbsp thyme leaves
500 g / 1 lb / 2 cups floury potatoes, peeled
2 tbsp butter, melted
2 tbsp vegetable oil
8 figs, cut into thin wedges
coriander (cilantro) sprigs, to decorate

- Preheat the oven to 200°C (180°C fan) / 400F / gas 6.
- Place the chicken in a roasting tin, season well, drizzle with olive oil and roast for 25–30 minutes until golden and cooked.
- Grate the potatoes. Toss with the melted butter and seasoning, ensuring they are thoroughly coated.
- Heat the vegetable oil in a large frying pan, then divide the mixture roughly into 8. Add the mixture in heaped spoonfuls a few at a time to the pan, pressing them down flat with a spatula. Cook over a medium heat for about 10 minutes until the base is brown.
- Run the spatula or a palette knife underneath to loosen, then turn the rösti over to cook the other side. Cook for a further 5–10 minutes until browned and crisp, then remove to kitchen towel to drain and repeat until all the rösti are cooked. Keep warm in the oven.
- For the last 5 minutes of cooking, add halved figs to the roasting tin with the chicken to warm through, then remove and leave to rest for 5 minutes.
- Place 2 rösti on each plate. Slice the chicken at an angle and sit on top, then spoon round the figs and roasting juices. Decorate with coriander sprigs.

299

SERVES 6

Indian Chicken Frittata

- Preheat the oven to 180°C (160°C fan) / 350F / gas 4.
- Combine the chopped chicken and cooked peas in a bowl.
- Beat the eggs with the creme fraîche in a large bowl.
- Add the eggs into the chicken and peas and season then mix together carefully. Add the spices and paneer if using.
- Oil a large ovenproof frying pan or round cake tin, then pour the mixture in, scatter with almonds and bake in the oven for about 35 minutes until puffed and golden. The egg should be cooked through.
- Cut the frittata into wedges and serve warm or cold.

PREPARATION TIME 10 MINUTES

COOKING TIME 35 MINUTES

INGREDIENTS

2 chicken breasts, cooked and chopped
150 g / 5 oz / ⅔ cup frozen peas, cooked
8 eggs
1 tbsp creme fraîche
100 g / 3 ½ oz / ½ cup paneer, optional
½ bunch coriander (cilantro), chopped
½ tsp turmeric
½ tbsp garam masala
2 tbsp flaked (slivered) almonds
olive oil
salt and pepper

Indian Chicken and Potato Frittata

300

- Bulk this up by adding 2 potatoes, chopped and steamed. Or green beans with cauliflower florets, chopped and steamed.

301

SERVES 2–4

Herby Chicken Salad

- Poach the chicken breasts in simmering water for about 20 minutes until cooked through. Set aside to rest, then shred finely.
- Tip the chicken into a large salad bowl and toss with the herbs, capers and seasoning.
- Whisk together the lemon juice and mustard, then whisk in the oil to make an emulsion.
- Toss the salad with the dressing and serve while still warm.

PREPARATION TIME 10 MINUTES

COOKING TIME 20 MINUTES

INGREDIENTS

4 chicken breasts, skinned
1 bunch parsley, roughly chopped
60 g / 2 oz / ¼ cup capers, drained
1 bunch chives, chopped
salt and pepper
½ lemon, juiced
1 tbsp Dijon mustard
80 ml / 2 ½ fl. oz / ⅓ cup extra virgin olive oil

Herby Chicken and Potato Salad

302

- Add boiled potatoes to the salad.

303

SERVES 4

Roast Chicken Legs with Sugar Snaps

PREPARATION TIME 10 MINUTES

COOKING TIME 30 MINUTES

INGREDIENTS

4 chicken legs
2 tbsp thyme leaves
4 tbsp olive oil
salt and pepper
250 g / 9 oz / 1 cup sugar snap peas
150 g / 5 oz / ⅔ cup pancetta, diced
1 clove of garlic, finely sliced
½ lemon, zested
1 tbsp tarragon leaves
1 red chilli (chili), deseeded and diced

- Preheat the oven to 200°C (180°C fan) / 400F / gas 6.
- Rub the chicken legs with thyme and seasoning, drizzle with half the oil and roast in the oven for about 30 minutes until golden and cooked through.
- Meanwhile steam the sugar snap peas over simmering water for 4–5 minutes until crisp-tender.
- Heat the remaining oil in a pan and fry the pancetta until the fat starts to run, then add the garlic and chilli and cook for 1 minute. Add the steamed sugar snaps, lemon zest and tarragon and toss to coat.
- Serve the chicken legs on top of the sugar snap pea mix.

Roast Chicken Legs with Croutons

304

- Add 1 ciabatta loaf torn into bite-size pieces around the chicken legs to soak up all the juices.

305

SERVES 4–6

Fruity Roast Chicken

PREPARATION TIME 15 MINUTES

COOKING TIME
1 HOUR 30 MINUTES

INGREDIENTS

1 oven ready chicken
500 g / 1 lb / 2 cups highly-flavoured sausages
75 g / 2 ½ oz / ⅓ cup breadcrumbs
1 apple, peeled, cored and diced
150 g / 5 oz / ⅔ cup dried apricots, chopped
2 tbsp thyme leaves
3 cloves of garlic, crushed
salt and pepper
40 g / 1 oz butter, softened
250 g / 9 oz / 1 cup couscous
250 ml / 9 fl. oz / 1 cup chicken or vegetable stock
60 g / 2 oz / ½ cup flaked (slivered) almonds
squeeze of lemon juice

- Preheat the oven to 220°C (200°C fan) / 425F / gas 7.
- Slit the skins of the sausage and squeeze the flesh into a bowl. Mix well with the breadcrumbs, apple, apricots, thyme, garlic and a little seasoning and spoon into the cavity of the chicken.
- Place the chicken in a roasting tin. Season, smear with butter and roast in the oven for 20 minutes then reduce the heat to 180°C (160°C fan) / 350F / gas 4 and cook for 1 hour or until the juices run clear.
- While the chicken is resting place the cous cous in a bowl, cover with the hot stock and cling film the bowl. Leave for 10 minutes or so until tender, then fork through the grains and add the lemon.
- Serve the chicken on top of the couscous, scattered with flaked almonds.

Fruity Roast Chicken with Rice

306

- Serve on a bed of boiled rice instead of couscous.

SERVES 4

Chicken and Coleslaw Burger

Chicken and Coleslaw Pitta

308

- Replace the burger bun with a pitta bread.

Indian Chicken Burgers

309

- Add a little chopped green chilli and a tsp of garam masala to the burger mix.

PREPARATION TIME 20 MINUTES

COOKING TIME 8–10 MINUTES

INGREDIENTS

500 g / 1 lb / 2 cups minced chicken
salt and pepper
1 lemon, zested
1 egg, beaten
½ red cabbage, cored
1 carrot, peeled and shredded
1 red onion, peeled and chopped
2 celery stalks, sliced
2 tbsp olive oil
4 burger buns
4 iceberg lettuce leaves, shredded
½ lime, juiced
2 tbsp sunflower oil
1 tbsp white wine vinegar

- Mix the chicken with the pepper, salt and lemon zest until thoroughly mixed. Pour in enough beaten egg to bind, but don't let the mixture get too wet. With wet hands, form the mixture into 8 small or 4 large burgers.

- Chill in the refrigerator for 30 minutes

- Meanwhile process the cabbage and onion in a food processor until finely shredded. Tip into a bowl, mix with the lime juice, sunflower oil and vinegar. Toss together the carrot and celery.

- Cook the burgers in a little olive oil for 3–4 minutes per side, depending on thickness.

- Split and lightly toast the burger buns, then spoon the lettuce and slaw onto the bottom half of each bun. Top with a burger and some carrot mix, sandwich and eat.

310

SERVES 4–6

Chicken Pastries

PREPARATION TIME 30 MINUTES

COOKING TIME 20 MINUTES

....

INGREDIENTS

4 tbsp olive oil
1 onion, peeled and thickly sliced
2 garlic cloves, finely chopped
2 chicken breasts, skinned and thickly sliced
½ tsp ground cinnamon
½ tsp ground cumin
½ tsp ground coriander (cilantro)
100 g / 3 ½ oz / ½ cup almonds, toasted
8 pieces roasted red pepper from a jar
salt and pepper
12–16 sheets filo pastry
120 g / 4 oz / ½ cup butter, melted
1 egg yolk, beaten
green salad, to serve

- Preheat the oven to 200°C (180°C fan) / 400F / gas 6.
- Heat the oil in a pan and sweat the onion and garlic until softened and turning gold. Add the chicken, spices and almonds and sauté until cooked through. Set aside to cool.
- Keeping the remaining filo sheets covered with a damp tea towel, remove one at a time from the pack and brush with melted butter before using.
- Place 2 sheets of pastry on a surface, brush each with melted butter, then place a roasted pepper piece on top. Spoon a little of the chicken mixture onto the pepper. Wrap the pastry around to enclose the filling. Repeat until all the filling and pastry is used up.
- Brush the tops with a little egg yolk, then bake in the oven for 15–20 minutes or until the pastry is crisp and golden. Serve with green salad.

Chicken Aubergine Pastries

311

- You could use the same method with long tender slices of cooked aubergine instead of the peppers.

312

SERVES 4–6

Roast Chicken with Pastis and Fennel

PREPARATION TIME 20 MINUTES

COOKING TIME
1 HOUR 30 MINUTES

....

INGREDIENTS

1 oven-ready chicken
40 g / 1 oz butter, softened
salt and pepper
4 thyme sprigs
½ lemon
3 fennel bulbs, halved
1 head garlic, halved
60 ml / 2 fl. oz / ¼ cup olive oil
100 ml / 3 ½ fl. oz / ½ cup Pastis (or vermouth if you can't find it)
200 ml / 7 fl. oz / ¾ cup chicken stock
handful black olives

- Preheat oven to 220°C (200°C fan) / 425F / gas 7.
- Smear the chicken with the butter and season generously. Stuff the cavity with thyme and the lemon half, place in a roasting tin and roast for 20 minutes.
- After 20 minutes lower the heat to 180°C (160°C fan) / 350F / gas 4 and add the fennel, garlic and drizzle over the oil and Pastis. Return to the oven for another hour or until the chicken is cooked through and the juices run clear when pierced with a toothpick.
- Transfer the chicken and vegetables to a serving platter and loosely cover with foil. Place the roasting tin on the hob and deglaze the pan with a wooden spoon, adding the stock. Simmer for 10–15 minutes until reduced and syrupy, adjust the seasoning and add the olives.
- Serve the chicken with the vegetables and the sauce.

Lemony Chicken with Fennel

313

- Adding a halved lemon to the roasting tin will really intensify the lemon flavours in this dish and you won't need so much stock.

314

SERVES 4

Chicken with Honey, Tomato and Almonds

- Heat the oil and cook the chicken briskly until golden, then reduce the heat and add the onion and spices and cook until the onion has softened.
- Stir in the tomatoes, stock and honey and simmer uncovered for 10–15 minutes until the sauce has reduced and the chicken has cooked.
- Stir through the almonds and season.

PREPARATION TIME 10 MINUTES

COOKING TIME 20 MINUTES

INGREDIENTS

3 tbsp olive oil
4 chicken thighs, skinned, deboned and diced
1 onion, peeled and finely sliced
1 tsp ground cumin
1 tsp ground coriander (cilantro)
1 tsp paprika
3 ripe tomatoes, thickly sliced
250 ml / 9 fl. oz / 1 cup chicken stock
2–3 tbsp runny honey
60 g / 2 oz / ⅓ cup whole skinned almonds
salt and pepper

Chicken with Aubergine and Almonds

315

- Aubergines go well with all the main flavourings in this dish and would add bulk and flavour.

316

SERVES 4

Baked Chicken with Yoghurt and Lemon

- Preheat the oven to 180°C (160°C fan) / 350F / gas 4.
- Place the chicken thighs skin side up in a roasting tin, surround with the lemon slices, drizzle with oil and season. Pour in the stock and wine and roast for 30 minutes or until the chicken is cooked through and the liquid reduced.
- Remove the chicken and lemon slices to a plate then tip the sauce into a pan. Simmer until reduced by a third or to your liking. Taste and see how intense you want the flavours, then remove from the heat and stir in the yoghurt. Do not reheat. Season and pour over the chicken.

PREPARATION TIME 5 MINUTES

COOKING TIME 40 MINUTES

INGREDIENTS

4–6 chicken thighs, skin on
4 tbsp olive oil
salt and pepper
½ lemon, sliced
200 ml / 7 fl. oz / ¾ cup chicken stock
100 ml / 3 ½ fl. oz / ½ cup dry white wine
150 ml / 5 fl. oz / ⅔ cup plain yoghurt

Herby Baked Chicken

317

- Parsley, basil, thyme and tarragon would all work well finely chopped and added to the sauce with the yoghurt.

318

SERVES 2

Honey Lime Chicken

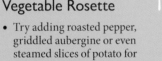

Lime Chicken with Vegetable Rosette

 319

- Try adding roasted pepper, griddled aubergine or even steamed slices of potato for colour and variation.

Honey Lime Chicken Kebabs

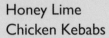 320

- Thread chunks of chicken coated the same way onto skewers and barbecue.

PREPARATION TIME 10 MINUTES

COOKING TIME 20 MINUTES

....

INGREDIENTS

2 chicken breasts
3 tbsp olive oil
2 tbsp runny honey
1 lime, juiced
salt and pepper
2 beef tomatoes, thickly sliced
1 courgette (zucchini), thickly sliced
1 lime, thinly sliced

- Preheat the oven to 200°C (180°C fan) / 400F / gas 6.
- Coat the chicken in 1 tbsp oil, honey and lime juice and season, then roast in the oven for 20 minutes until cooked through. Set aside to rest.
- Meanwhile heat a griddle pan to hot. Brush the tomatoes and courgette with oil and griddle over high heat until tender, but try to keep the tomatoes holding their shape.
- Thickly slice the chicken and serve on a plate interleaved with lime slices. Layer the courgette and tomato slices into a tower and serve.

Chicken with Raisin Couscous

321

SERVES 4

- Heat the oil in a pan and cook the chicken with the garlic until golden and cooked through. Season and set aside.
- Place the couscous in a bowl, add the raisins, cover with the hot stock and clingfilm the bowl. Leave for 10 minutes or so until tender, then fork through the grains and add the lemon, parsley and pine nuts.
- Serve the couscous on a large serving platter topped with the cooked chicken.

PREPARATION TIME 10 MINUTES

COOKING TIME 10–15 MINUTES

INGREDIENTS

4 chicken thighs, skinned, deboned
and cut into chunks
2 tbsp olive oil
1 clove of garlic, crushed
salt and pepper
250 g / 9 oz / 1 cup couscous
250 ml / 9 fl. oz / 1 cup chicken or
vegetable stock
60 g / 2 oz / ⅓ cup raisins
squeeze of lemon juice
1 bunch parsley, roughly chopped
2 tbsp pine nuts, toasted

Chicken with Mushroom Couscous

322

- Replace the raisins with mushrooms.

Grilled Chicken with Bananas and Lime Rice

323

SERVES 2

- Tip the rice into a pan with the lime zest and cover with water. Cook with the lid on for 12–14 minutes until cooked and tender, then drain thoroughly. Return to the pan, toss with lime juice, almonds and salt.
- Brush the chicken breasts with honey, oil and seasoning and griddle over high heat skin side down until golden and stripy. Turn over, reduce the heat and cook for another 6–8 minutes until cooked through.
- Griddle the bananas in their skins until blackened and the insides softened. Carefully peel and slice.
- Serve the chicken with the rice and top with the bananas and lime slices.

PREPARATION TIME 5 MINUTES

COOKING TIME 20 MINUTES

INGREDIENTS

120 g / 4 oz / ½ cup basmati rice
juice and zest of 1 lime
60 g / 2 oz / ½ cup flaked (slivered)
almonds, toasted
2 chicken breasts, skin on
1 tbsp honey
2 tbsp olive oil
salt and pepper
2 bananas, in their peel
1 lime, sliced

Chicken with Grilled Courgette

324

- Try substituting the bananas for courgettes and cook in the same way.

325

SERVES 2

Chicken, Feta and Beetroot Salad

PREPARATION TIME 10 MINUTES

COOKING TIME 20 MINUTES

INGREDIENTS

2 chicken breasts, skin on
salt and pepper
2 tbsp olive oil
1 tbsp rosemary leaves, finely
chopped
2 whole beetroot, ready cooked
and peeled (not in vinegar)
150 g / 5 oz / ⅔ cup feta cheese,
crumbled
1 tbsp balsamic vinegar
3 tbsp extra virgin olive oil
½ orange, zested
mixed salad leaves

- Preheat the oven to 200°C (180°C fan) / 400F / gas 6.
- Season the chicken and rub in the rosemary leaves, drizzle with oil and roast in the oven for 20 minutes until cooked. Set aside to rest for 10 minutes.
- Meanwhile, slice the beetroot into wedges and place in a bowl with the salad leaves.
- Whisk together the balsamic, extra virgin olive oil, orange zest and seasoning and toss the salad lightly in the dressing.
- Slice the chicken, sit it on top of the salad and crumble over the feta cheese.

Chicken Salad
with Mustard Dressing

326

- A sharper mustard dressing would also go well: whisk 1 tbsp Dijon with 1 tbsp red wine vinegar, olive oil and seasoning.

327

SERVES 4

Japanese Fried Chicken

PREPARATION TIME 10 MINUTES

COOKING TIME 15–20 MINUTES

INGREDIENTS

4 chicken breasts, skinned and each
cut into 3 pieces
3 tbsp soy sauce
1 tbsp teriyaki sauce
100 g / 3 ½ oz / ½ cup plain
(all purpose) flour
2 eggs, beaten
200 g / 7 oz / ¾ cup panko crumbs
vegetable oil
finely sliced cucumber, to serve

- Place the chicken in a bowl with the soy and teriyaki. Refrigerate for at least 2 hours or even overnight.
- Dip the chicken pieces one at a time into the flour, egg then panko crumbs and lay on a rack to dry slightly.
- Heat 1 cm depth oil in a pan and fry the chicken in batches until golden on both sides and cooked through.
- Serve hot or cold with cucumber.

Fried Chicken with Dipping Sauce

328

- Try mixing a little rice wine (mirin) with teriyaki and soy sauce and a little chilli.

Chicken Roasted with Thyme and Lemon

Chicken with Thyme and Lime

330

- Replace the lemon with a lime.

Thyme Chicken with Basil Mash

331

- Stir chopped basil into very creamy mashed potato to serve alongside.

PREPARATION TIME 5 MINUTES

COOKING TIME 30–35 MINUTES

INGREDIENTS

4 chicken legs, skin on
2–3 tbsp olive oil
1 tbsp butter
1 lemon, zested and halved
2 tsp dried thyme
salt and pepper
100 ml / 3 ½ fl. oz / ½ cup white wine

- Preheat the oven to 200°C (180°C fan) / 400F / gas 6.
- Place the chicken legs in a snug fitting roasting tin. Smear over the oil and butter and season with salt, pepper and thyme. Squeeze over the juice from the lemon and add the empty halves to the tin. Sprinkle the lemon zest on top.
- Roast in the oven for about 30–35 minutes until golden and cooked through.
- Transfer the chicken to a plate to rest, loosely covered with foil. Place the tin on the hob, deglaze with the white wine and simmer the juices for a couple of minutes to reduce and intensify. Season.
- Serve the legs with the roasting juices spooned over.

332

SERVES 4

Chicken Escalope with Exotic Fruit

Grilled Kebabs

333

- Place the kebabs on the griddle at the same time as the chicken and turn frequently.

Stuffed Cherry Tomatoes and Chicken Escalope

334

- Hollow out the tomatoes and stuff a little cheese inside before cooking.

PREPARATION TIME 15 MINUTES

COOKING TIME 15 MINUTES

INGREDIENTS

4 chicken breasts, skinned
salt and pepper
3 tbsp olive oil
½ lemon, juiced
chopped parsley
16 cherry tomatoes
3–4 star fruit, sliced
1 orange, sliced
1 lime, cut into wedges

- Place the chicken breasts one at a time between 2 pieces of cling film and bash with a rolling pin until about 1 cm (½ in) thick. Transfer to a plate, rub with 2 tbsp oil and season.

- Heat a griddle pan until very hot and cook the escalopes 2 at a time until stripy and golden, then turn and cook the other side, about 2–3 minutes per side. Transfer to a plate and keep warm.

- Meanwhile toss the cherry tomatoes with the remaining oil and parsley and thread onto wooden skewers.

- Briefly griddle the star fruit, orange slices and lime wedges until just starting to turn golden.

- Squeeze a little lemon juice over the chicken and serve with the skewers and fruit.

335

SERVES 2 Parsley-stuffed Chicken with Chips

- Preheat the oven to 190°C (170°C fan) / 375F / gas 5.
- Place the chicken between 2 pieces of cling film and bash out with a rolling pin to about 1.5 cm thick.
- Pulse the parsley, pine nuts, garlic and oil in a processor until combined but not mushy. Divide equally between the chicken breasts, spooning the filling down the centre. Roll the chicken into a sausage-shape and tie with string to secure. Place in a roasting tin, season and roast for about 15 minutes until cooked.
- To make the chips, soak well in cold water to remove the starch then dry thoroughly.
- Bring a pan a third full of oil to 140°C / 275F and plunge in the chips, and cook for 10 minutes until pale. Remove, drain on kitchen paper.
- Heat the oil to 180°C / 350F and plunge the chips back in until golden and crisp. Remove to kitchen paper, season well and serve with the sliced stuffed chicken.

Pesto-stuffed Chicken 336

- Replace the stuffing with pesto.

PREPARATION TIME 20 MINUTES

COOKING TIME 20 MINUTES

INGREDIENTS

2 chicken breasts, skinned
1 bunch parsley, chopped
4 tbsp pine nuts, lightly toasted
1 clove of garlic, crushed
2–3 tbsp extra virgin olive oil
4 large baking potatoes, peeled and cut into 1 cm thick batons
vegetable oil
salt

337

SERVES 4–6 All-in-one Roast Chicken

- Preheat the oven to 200°C (180°C fan) / 400F / gas 6.
- Place the chicken in a roasting tin. Using the handle of a teaspoon, gently loosen the skin from the meat, using the spoon to create pockets.
- Mix the butter with the parsley, seasoning and lemon zest.
- Push the butter into the pockets under the skin, using your fingers to massage it out and cover the breast.
- Drizzle the skin with oil and season, then roast in the oven for 20 minutes.
- Reduce the heat to 180°C (160°C fan) / 350F / gas 4.
- Toss the bread with the chicken juices in the bottom of the tray, drizzle with a little oil and roast for 1 hour or until the juices run clear when pierced with a toothpick. 5 minutes before the end of cooking, toss in the olives.
- Leave to rest for 10 minutes before carving.

Chicken with Roast Tomatoes 338

- Halve a few tomatoes and roast alongside the chicken for extra flavour.

PREPARATION TIME 10 MINUTES

COOKING TIME
1 HOUR 30 MINUTES

INGREDIENTS

1 oven-ready chicken

FOR THE BUTTER
½ bunch parsley, finely chopped
150 g / 5 oz / ⅔ cup butter, softened
salt and pepper
½ lemon, zested
1 baguette, torn into small-ish pieces
olive oil
60 g / 2 oz / ⅓ cup green olives, stoned

339

SERVES 4

Chicken Burgers with Pepper and Basil

PREPARATION TIME 10 MINUTES

COOKING TIME 8–10 MINUTES

INGREDIENTS

500 g / 1 lb / 2 cups minced chicken
1 bunch basil leaves, finely chopped
1 tsp Espelette pepper
salt
1 lemon, zested
1 egg, beaten
vegetable oil
lemon wedges, to serve

- Mix the chicken with the basil, pepper, salt and lemon zest until thoroughly mixed.
- Pour in enough beaten egg to bind, but don't let the mixture get too wet. With wet hands, form the mixture into 8 small or 4 large burgers.
- Chill in the refrigerator for 30 minutes.
- Cook in a little oil for 3–4 minutes per side, depending on thickness. Serve with lemon wedges.

Cheesy Chicken Burgers with Pepper

340

- Add a handful of grated cheese to the burger mix.

341

SERVES 4

Grilled Mustard Chicken Legs

PREPARATION TIME 5 MINUTES

COOKING TIME 10–15 MINUTES

INGREDIENTS

4 chicken legs, skin on, boned out
2 tbsp olive oil
2 tbsp Dijon mustard
small handful thyme leaves
½ lemon, juiced
salt and pepper

- Mix together the oil, mustard, thyme and some seasoning and thoroughly coat the chicken legs in the mixture.
- Grill or griddle for 10–15 minutes, turning regularly until the chicken is golden and cooked through.
- Squeeze over a little lemon, slice and serve.

Grilled Honey Mustard Chicken

342

- Use grain mustard and add 1 tbsp runny honey to ring the changes.

SERVES 2

Chicken with Mushroom Sauce

Chicken with Dried Mushrooms

344

- Soak dried wild mushrooms in hot water for 15 minutes beforehand and use a little of the water in the sauce to intensify the flavour.

Chicken with Cheese Polenta

345

- Serve with cooked polenta mixed with 200 g / 7 oz / 1 cup grated Cheddar cheese.

PREPARATION TIME 10 MINUTES

COOKING TIME 40 MINUTES

INGREDIENTS

40 g / 1 oz butter
2 chicken breasts
1 shallot, finely chopped
2 cloves of garlic, finely sliced
100 g / 3 ½ oz / ½ cup button or chestnut mushrooms, sliced
100 g / 3 ½ oz / ½ cup wild mushrooms, cleaned
100 ml / 3 ½ fl. oz / ½ cup dry white wine
150 ml / 5 fl. oz / ⅔ cup double (heavy) cream
salt and pepper
120 g / 4 oz / ½ cup white and wild rice, to serve

- Cook the white and wild rice according to packet instructions, drain and keep warm.

- Heat the butter in a pan and cook the chicken skin side down until golden. Turn over and cook on the other side for 5–6 minutes until cooked through. Remove from the pan with a slotted spoon and keep warm.

- If the butter has burnt, wipe out the pan and replace with more. Sweat the shallot and garlic without colouring. Add the mushrooms and season, then sauté until any excess liquid has evaporated, then deglaze the pan with the white wine. Reduce until syrupy then add the cream and bubble up.

- Serve the chicken sliced with sauce spooned over and wild rice to accompany.

346

SERVES 6

Chicken and Courgette Quiche

PREPARATION TIME 50 MINUTES

COOKING TIME 1 HOUR

INGREDIENTS

2 chicken breasts, skinned and diced
30 g / 1 oz butter
1 courgette (zucchini), finely diced
½ bunch tarragon, finely chopped
100 g / 3 ½ oz / ½ cup Gruyère
cheese, grated
2 eggs + 1 egg yolk
300 ml / 10 fl. oz / 1 ¼ cups double
(heavy) cream
salt and pepper

FOR THE QUICHE PASTRY

110 g / 3 ½ oz / ½ cup plain
(all purpose) flour
50 g / 1 ¾ oz / ¼ cup cold, diced
butter
pinch salt
cold water, to mix

- Preheat the oven to 200°C (180°C fan) / 400F / gas 6.
- Rub the butter into the flour with the salt until you have coarse breadcrumbs. Add water a little at a time and mix until the mixture just comes together. Form into a ball, cover with clingfilm and refrigerate for 20–30 minutes.
- Fry the chicken and courgettes in the butter until golden. Set aside to cool.
- Roll out the pastry and press it gently into a lightly greased flan tin. Prick all over with a fork and bake in the oven on a baking sheet for 20 minutes until pale gold.
- Spoon the chicken and courgettes evenly over the pastry base. Whisk together the eggs, cream, cheese and tarragon and season, then pour in.
- Bake in the oven for 25–30 minutes until just set. Leave to cool before serving.

Chicken and Ham Quiche

 347

- Chopped ham adds depth of flavour.

348

SERVES 4

Chicken Basquaise

PREPARATION TIME 10 MINUTES

COOKING TIME 30 MINUTES

INGREDIENTS

2 tbsp olive oil
4 chicken thighs
1 onion, chopped
2 cloves of garlic, chopped
1 red pepper, deseeded and sliced
1 green pepper, deseeded and sliced
1 yellow pepper, deseeded and sliced
6 ripe vine tomatoes, cored and
chopped
2 bay leaves
1 tsp sugar
2 tsp smoked paprika
salt and pepper
chopped fresh parsley

- Heat the oil in a pan and brown the thighs until golden. Remove to a plate and set aside.
- Add the onion and garlic and cook gently until golden, then add the chicken back to the pan and add the peppers and tomatoes, bay leaves, sugar, paprika and seasoning and allow to simmer for about 10–15 minutes until all is cooked through. Add a splash of water if it starts to look dry. Adjust the seasoning.
- Serve hot with rice or crusty bread, scattered with parsley.

Chicken and Chorizo Basquaise

 349

- Add 100 g / 3 ½ oz / ½ cup chopped chorizo with the vegetables for a real punch of smoky flavour.

350

SERVES 4–6 Creamy Chicken Lasagne

- Heat 40 g butter in a pan and add the vegetables and chicken and cook gently for 10 minutes. Season.
- Add the wine and stir for about 5 minutes until it has evaporated. Add the herbs and set aside.
- Meanwhile make the béchamel sauce: heat the butter in a pan until foaming, then stir in the flour to make a paste. Whisk in the milk a little at a time.
- Add the bay leaf and simmer for 10 minutes, whisking frequently. Season and add freshly grated nutmeg. Stir the chicken mixture into ⅔ of the béchamel.
- Preheat the oven to 190°C (170°C fan) / 375F / gas 5.
- Spread half the remaining béchamel in the base of a baking dish, then top with 4 lasagne sheets. Add a third of the chicken mix, then 4 more sheets. Repeat chicken and pasta layers twice more. Finish with the remaining béchamel and Parmesan.
- Bake in the oven for about 40 minutes until tender.

Chicken and Tomato Lasagne 351

- Add 6 chopped tomatoes to the mix for fresh flavour.

PREPARATION TIME 30 MINUTES

COOKING TIME 40 MINUTES

INGREDIENTS

40 g / 1 oz butter
1 onion, peeled and finely chopped
1 carrot, peeled and diced
1 celery stick, finely chopped
250 g / 9 oz / 1 cup mushrooms, chopped
500 g / 1 lb / 2 cups chicken meat, diced
200 ml / 7 fl. oz / ¾ cup dry white wine
1 bunch tarragon or parsley, chopped
salt and pepper
12 fresh lasagne sheets
2 tbsp Parmesan, grated
2 tbsp butter
2 tbsp plain (all purpose) flour
700 ml / 1 ¼ pints / 2 ¾ cups milk
1 bay leaf
nutmeg

352

SERVES 4 Chicken, Lemon and Olive Fricassee

- Heat the olive oil in a casserole and brown the chicken thighs until golden all over.
- Add the onions and carrots to the pan and cook for 10 minutes until softened. Add the bay, lemons and stock, cover with a lid and cook for 30 minutes or until the chicken is cooked through and the carrots are tender.
- Stir through the caperberries and olives, season carefully and serve.

Chicken Fricassee with Green Beans 353

- Add 100 g / 3 ½ oz / ½ cup green beans to the stock for added colour.

PREPARATION TIME 10 MINUTES

COOKING TIME 45 MINUTES

INGREDIENTS

2 tbsp olive oil
4 chicken thighs, skin on
1 onion, peeled and chopped
8 baby carrots, scrubbed
2 bay leaves
2 preserved lemons, chopped
300 ml / 10 fl. oz / 1 ½ cups chicken stock
2 tbsp caperberries, drained
60 g / 2 oz / ⅓ cup green olives
salt and pepper

354

SERVES 2

Chicken Noodles

PREPARATION TIME 10 MINUTES

COOKING TIME 10 MINUTES

INGREDIENTS

2 tbsp vegetable oil
1 onion, peeled and finely sliced
1 clove of garlic, finely sliced
1 cm piece fresh ginger, finely sliced
1 red pepper, deseeded and finely sliced
1 green pepper, deseeded and finely sliced
2 chicken thighs, skinned, deboned and chopped
3–4 tbsp soy sauce
2 tbsp oyster sauce
100 ml / 3 ½ fl. oz / ½ cup chicken stock
2 nests noodles
1 tbsp sesame oil
1 tbsp Szechuan peppercorns, crushed (optional)

- Heat the oil in a wok until nearly smoking then stir fry the onion, ginger and garlic until golden.
- Add the vegetables and stir fry until just tender, then add the chicken and cook through.
- Meanwhile cook the noodles in boiling salted water according to packet instructions, then drain.
- Add the sauces and stock to the pan and bubble up, then add the cooked noodles and sesame oil.
- Serve topped with the crushed peppercorns.

Quick Chicken Noodles

 355

- This is already pretty speedy, but for a quicker version use grated carrot and courgette in place of the peppers and use pre-cooked chicken.

356

SERVES 6

Roast Chicken with Stuffing and Apples

PREPARATION TIME 20 MINUTES

COOKING TIME
1 HOUR 30 MINUTES

INGREDIENTS

1 oven-ready chicken
2 tbsp oil
salt and pepper
6 eating apples, halved

FOR THE STUFFING
2 tbsp butter
250 g / 9 oz / 1 cup mushrooms, finely chopped
1 onion, finely chopped
1 clove of garlic, chopped
1 lemon, zested
½ bunch parsley
1 slice bread, soaked in milk
1 egg, beaten

- Preheat the oven to 190°C (170°C fan) / 375F / gas 5.
- Heat the butter in a pan and cook the mushrooms and onions until soft. Add the garlic and stir well.
- Transfer to a bowl and mix in the zest, parsley, crumble in the bread then mix in the egg. Use your hands to combine everything.
- Spoon the stuffing into the cavity of the chicken and place in a roasting tin. Place the apple halves around the outside. Season, drizzle with oil and roast in the oven for about 1 ½ hours until the juices run clear when pierced with a toothpick.
- Leave the chicken to rest for 10 minutes before carving.

Roast Chicken with Pears

357

- Replace the apples with pears.

358

SERVES 4

Chicken with Herby Tortilla

Tomato and Herb Tortilla

359

- Halved cherry tomatoes would add colour and freshness to the tortilla and make a good foil to the savoury chicken.

Chicken and Potato Tortilla

360

- Add diced steamed white or sweet potato to the egg mix before baking.

PREPARATION TIME 15 MINUTES

COOKING TIME 35 MINUTES

INGREDIENTS

6 eggs
1 tbsp creme fraiche
½ bunch coriander (cilantro) chopped
½ bunch parsley, chopped
olive oil
salt and pepper
4 chicken legs
2 tbsp olive oil
½ bunch tarragon, chopped
200 ml / 7 fl. oz / ⅔ cup dry white wine
halved green tomatoes, to serve

- Preheat the oven to 190°C (170°C fan) / 375F / gas 5.
- Beat the eggs with the creme fraiche in a large bowl. Add the coriander and parsley and season then mix together carefully.
- Oil a large frying pan, then pour the mixture in and bake for about 35 minutes until puffed and golden. The egg should be cooked through.
- Meanwhile, roast the chicken legs in the oven drizzled with oil and seasoned. They should take the same amount of time.
- Remove the legs to a plate to rest. Place the tin on the hob and deglaze with the white wine, scraping with a wooden spoon, and stir in the tarragon. Season.
- Cut the tortilla into wedges and serve warm or cold alongside the chicken and tarragon jus with green tomatoes.

361

SERVES 6

Guinea Fowl with Chanterelle Stuffing

PREPARATION TIME 20 MINUTES

COOKING TIME

1 HOUR 30 MINUTES

....

INGREDIENTS

1 guinea fowl
40 g / 1 oz butter
salt and pepper

FOR THE STUFFING

2 tbsp butter
200 g / 7 oz / ¾ cup chicken livers, trimmed
500 g / 1lb / 2 cups chanterelles
1 onion, finely chopped
1 clove of garlic, chopped
½ bunch thyme
1 slice bread, soaked in milk
1 egg, beaten
fried chanterelles and sliced sausagemeat stuffing, to serve

- Preheat the oven to 200°C (180°C fan) / 400F / gas 6.
- Melt the butter in a pan and cook the chicken livers briskly until brown on the outside. Add the onion, garlic and chanterelles and sauté until softened, then stir in the thyme leaves and season.
- Spoon into a bowl, crumble in the bread and stir in the egg until thoroughly combined.
- Stuff the cavity of the guinea fowl and place in a roasting tin. Roast for 20 minutes then turn the oven down to 180°C (160°C fan) / 350F / gas 4.
- Roast for a further 45 minutes then check to see if the juices run clear when pierced with a toothpick. If not return to the oven for 10 minutes.
- Rest for 15–20 minutes before carving, then serve with fried chanterelles and extra sausagemeat stuffing.

Guinea Fowl with Bacon Stuffing   **362**

- Add chopped streaky bacon and prunes to the stuffing mixture for richness.

363

SERVES 4

Crunchy Asian Chicken Salad

PREPARATION TIME 25 MINUTES

....

INGREDIENTS

2 chicken breasts, cooked
2 carrots, peeled and cut into fine batons
½ white cabbage, cored and finely shredded
2 courgettes (zucchini), cut into fine batons
½ bunch coriander (cilantro), chopped
4 tbsp cashew nuts or peanuts, chopped
2 tbsp fish sauce
½ red chilli (chili), finely chopped
1 lime, juiced
1 tbsp soy sauce
1 tsp sugar

- Shred the chicken and toss in a large serving bowl with the vegetables and coriander.
- Add the nuts and toss again.
- Whisk together the fish sauce, chilli, lime, soy, sugar and taste. Adjust the seasoning if necessary.
- Spoon over the salad and toss thoroughly to coat. Leave for 5 minutes to soak up the flavours, then serve.

Asian Seafood Salad   **364**

- Add prawns, squid and even crab, all of which eat well with the dressing.

365

SERVES 4–6 # Pot Roast Chicken with Vegetables

- Preheat the oven to 200°C (180°C fan) / 400F / gas 6.
- Place the chicken in a casserole. Smear the butter over the skin, sprinkle with fennel seeds and seasoning. Roast in the oven for 20 minutes.
- Reduce the heat to 180°C (160°C fan) / 350F / gas 4.
- Add the vegetables to the pot with the wine, cover with a lid and return to the oven for 1 hour or until the chicken is cooked through. Remove the lid for 10 minutes to crisp the skin again if necessary.
- Serve in the pot at the table.

Pot Roast Chicken with Apples and Potatoes

366

- Try adding halved waxy potatoes, wedges of apple and cider in place of the wine.

PREPARATION TIME 10 MINUTES

COOKING TIME
1 HOUR 30 MINUTES

....

INGREDIENTS

1 oven-ready chicken
40 g / 1 oz butter, softened
1 tbsp fennel seeds
salt and pepper
1 head of broccoli, separated into florets
200 g / 7 oz / ¾ cup green beans
250 g / 9 oz / 1 cup mushrooms, sliced
1 red pepper, deseeded and finely diced
200 ml / 7 fl. oz / ¾ cup white wine

367

SERVES # Chicken, Almond and Honey Tart

- Preheat the oven to 200°C (180°C fan) / 400F / gas 6.
- Roll half the pastry out on a floured surface and use to line a pie dish, pushing into the corners. Prick the base all over with a fork and bake in the oven for 10 minutes until pale gold. Leave to cool.
- Meanwhile heat the oil in a pan and gently cook the onion and carrot until golden and sweet. Add the chicken and spices, increase the heat slightly and cook until the chicken is golden.
- Add the almonds and honey and stir well to combine. Tip into the pie dish, cover with the remaining puff pastry sheet, crimping well around the edges to seal. Brush with beaten egg and bake in the oven for 25–30 minutes until dark gold.
- Serve hot or cold.

Chicken and Chickpea Pie

368

- Adding a 400 g can of drained chickpeas would stretch this pie even further.

PREPARATION TIME 10 MINUTES

COOKING TIME 40–45 MINUTES

....

INGREDIENTS

2 sheets ready-rolled puff pastry
2 tbsp olive oil
1 onion, peeled and sliced
1 carrot, peeled and thinly sliced
4 chicken thighs, skinned, deboned and diced
1 tsp ground cumin
1 tsp ground coriander (cilantro)
100 g / 3 ½ oz / 1 cup ground almonds
2 tbsp runny honey
1 egg, beaten

369

SERVES 6

Mediterranean Chicken Tart

Mozzarella Chicken and Vegetable Tart

370

- Once the tart has nearly cooked, add slices of mozzarella to ooze slowly across the top.

Chicken and Parma Ham Tart

371

- Layer very thin slices of Parma ham on top before baking to crisp in the oven.

PREPARATION TIME 10 MINUTES

COOKING TIME 35–40 MINUTES

INGREDIENTS

1 sheet ready-rolled shortcrust pastry
1 egg, beaten

FOR THE FILLING
olive oil
1 onion, peeled and finely chopped
1 carrot, peeled and thinly sliced
2 cloves of garlic, finely sliced
200 g / 7 oz / ¾ cup mushrooms, quartered
1 aubergine, cut into thin rounds
2 courgettes, cut into thin rounds
1 jar roasted red peppers
2 chicken thighs, skinned, deboned and chopped
2 tbsp chopped fresh oregano
salt and pepper

- Preheat the oven to 180°C (160°C fan) / 350F / gas 4.
- Roll out the pastry and use to line a pie dish. Blind bake in the oven for 10 minutes until pale gold. Remove and leave to cool.
- Heat the oil in a pan and cook the onion and garlic until slightly golden. Add the mushrooms and fry until golden. Remove from the pan to a bowl with a slotted spoon.
- Add the aubergine and a little more oil and cook until tender, taking care to try to keep the sliced intact. Remove to kitchen paper. Repeat with the courgette and chicken.
- Arrange the vegetables, peppers and chicken in the pastry case then scatter with chopped oregano and seasoning.
- Bake in the oven for about 20 minutes until the pastry is golden. Serve warm.

372

SERVES 4

Chicken, Potato and Mushroom Pie

- Sieve flour and salt into a bowl, work in butter until the mix resembles breadcrumbs. Work in 2 tbsp water, bring mixture together to make a ball of dough. Wrap in cling film, refrigerate for 30 minutes.
- Preheat the oven to 200°C (180°C fan) / 400F / gas 6.
- Heat the butter in a pan and fry the chicken pieces until golden in patches. Remove with a slotted spoon.
- Sweat the shallot and mushrooms with the parsley. Return the chicken to pan, season and add potatoes.
- Divide the pastry in half. Roll one piece out on a floured surface to slightly larger than the pie dish and sit it in the base. Blind bake for 15 minutes.
- Tip chicken mixture into the pastry base. Roll the remaining pastry to slightly larger than the pie dish and sit on top of the filling.
- Brush with beaten egg, make a hole in the pastry to let the steam escape, bake in oven for 30 minutes.

PREPARATION TIME 35 MINUTES

COOKING TIME 45 MINUTES

INGREDIENTS

2 tbsp butter
3–4 chicken thighs, deboned and skinned, cut into chunks
1 shallot, finely chopped
200 g / 7 oz / ¾ cup chestnut mushrooms, sliced
3 large floury potatoes, peeled and diced, parboiled
¼ bunch parsley, chopped
salt and pepper
1 egg, beaten

FOR THE PASTRY

120 g / 4 oz / ½ cup plain (all purpose) flour
60 g / 2 oz / ¼ cup butter
pinch salt
cold water

Chicken, Swede and Mushroom Pie

373

- The earthy sweet flavour of swede makes a good alternative to potato.

374

SERVES 2

Grilled Chicken and Tofu Skewers

- Marinate the chicken and tofu with the rest of the ingredients for 30 minutes.
- Thread alternately onto soaked wooden skewers and griddle over high heat until stripy and cooked through - about 8 minutes.
- Serve with a squeeze of lemon juice.

PREPARATION TIME 5 MINUTES

COOKING TIME 8–10 MINUTES

INGREDIENTS

2 chicken breasts, skinned and cubed
200 g / 7 oz / ¾ cup firm tofu, cut into squares
½ lemon, juiced and zested
½ bunch mint leaves
1 tbsp olive oil
salt and pepper

Grilled Chicken and Halloumi Skewers

375

- Substitute the tofu for a pack of halloumi, cubed and cooked just the same.

376

SERVES 4

Chicken and Mango Fajitas

PREPARATION TIME 35 MINUTES

COOKING TIME 10–15 MINUTES

INGREDIENTS

4 chicken breasts, skinned and
thinly sliced
2 tsp paprika
2 tsp ground cumin
2 tsp ground coriander (cilantro)
pinch dried chilli (chili) flakes
salt and pepper
4 tbsp olive oil
1 mango, peeled, stoned and sliced
1 ½ limes, juiced
4 ripe tomatoes, cored and diced
2 tbsp extra virgin olive oil
hot sauce
3 spring onions (scallions),
finely chopped
8 tortilla wraps

- Coat the chicken in half the spices and leave to marinate for 30 minutes.
- Heat half the oil in a pan until nearly smoking, then cook the chicken until tender, then sprinkle over the rest of the spices.
- Stir briskly for 2–3 minutes until the chicken is just cooked through. Squeeze over ⅔ of the lime juice. Remove and keep warm.
- Toss the tomatoes in a bowl with oil, hot sauce to taste, spring onions, remaining lime juice and seasoning.
- Wipe out the chicken pan and use to warm the tortillas through.
- Serve the chicken with the mango slices to fill the tortillas and tomato salsa alongside.

Fajitas with Avocado and Tomato Salsa

377

- Avocado is the perfect accompaniment. Stir cubed avocado into the tomatoes for a creamy contrast.

378

SERVES 4

Sweet and Sour Chicken Fajitas

PREPARATION TIME 5 MINUTES

COOKING TIME 15–20 MINUTES

INGREDIENTS

1 tbsp vegetable oil
4 chicken breasts, skinned and cubed
1 onion, peeled and sliced
1 mango or ½ pineapple, diced
8 tortillas
lettuce leaves

FOR THE SAUCE
125 ml / 4 fl. oz / ½ cup pineapple
juice
splash dry sherry or Shaoxing
rice wine
2 tbsp ketchup
2 tbsp soy sauce
2 tbsp Chinese vinegar or red
wine vinegar
1 tsp cornflour (cornstarch)

- Heat the oil in a pan or wok and stir fry the chicken and onion until golden.
- Add the sauce ingredients and bubble up until thickened. Stir in the mango or pineapple.
- Warm the tortillas briefly in a dry pan.
- Wrap the chicken mix in the tortillas with lettuce leaves.

Sweet and Sour Fajitas with Rice

379

- Serve alongside Mexican fried rice.

380

SERVES 6

Chicken Cannelloni

Light Chicken Cannelloni

381

- Use canned tomatoes in place of the cream.

Chicken Lasagne

382

- Use lasagne sheets and layer with the chicken mix in a gratin dish, sprinkle with cheese and bake.

PREPARATION TIME 20 MINUTES

COOKING TIME 20 MINUTES

....

INGREDIENTS

3 tbsp olive oil
2 shallots, finely chopped
1 onion, finely chopped
1 clove of garlic, finely chopped
500 g / 1 lb / 2 cups wild mushrooms
4 chicken thighs, skinned, deboned and diced
1 bunch parsley, chopped
300 ml / 10 fl. oz / 1 ¼ cups double (heavy) cream
12–18 cannelloni tubes
40 g /1 oz butter
3 tbsp Parmesan, grated
salt and pepper

- Preheat the oven to 200°C (180°C fan) / 400F / gas 6.
- Heat the oil in a pan and add the shallot and onion. Cook for a few minutes, stirring regularly.
- Add the mushrooms, chicken and garlic and cook until the liquid has evaporated. Season, then add the parsley and half the double cream. Reduce until the cream has thickened, then remove from the heat.
- Cook the cannelloni tubes in boiling salted water according to packet instructions. Drain thoroughly and pat dry.
- Stuff the cannellonis with the chicken mixture, either use a piping bag or a teaspoon.
- Place in a buttered baking dish, pour over the remaining cream and sprinkle with Parmesan and a few dots of butter.
- Cook in the oven for 20 minutes then serve scattered with parsley.

383

SERVES 4

Chicken in Red Wine Mushroom Sauce

PREPARATION TIME 20 MINUTES

COOKING TIME 45 MINUTES

INGREDIENTS

50 g / 2 oz / ½ cup dried mushrooms
300 ml / 10 fl. oz / 1 ¼ cups chicken stock
2 tbsp olive oil
4 chicken legs, skin on
1 onion, peeled and finely chopped
2 cloves of garlic, finely chopped
100 g / 3 ½ oz / ½ cup chanterelles
200 ml / 7 fl. oz / ¾ cup red wine
¼ bunch parsley
salt and pepper
500 g / 1 lb / 2 cups ready made gnocchi
40 g / 1 oz butter

- Cut a slit in the side of each chicken breast, without cutting all the way through. Open out like a book.
- Heat the oil in a pan and brown the chicken legs on both sides, then remove and set aside.
- Add the onion and garlic and cook until softened, then add the chanterelles. Remove the dried mushrooms with a slotted spoon and add to the pan and cook all for 5–10 minutes until the mushrooms are tender.
- Deglaze with the red wine and reduce by half, then add the chicken stock, reserving the last little bit as there may be grit from the mushrooms. Add the parsley stalks and chicken back to the pan and simmer for 30 minutes until the chicken is cooked through.
- Meanwhile cook the gnocchi in boiling salted water according to packet instructions, then drain and toss with butter and seasoning.
- Serve alongside the chicken and mushroom sauce.

384

SERVES 4

Chicken Bouchees

PREPARATION TIME 10 MINUTES

COOKING TIME 20 MINUTES

INGREDIENTS

4 chicken breasts, skinned, deboned
4 slices ham
1 ball mozzarella, sliced
75 g / 2 ½ oz / ⅓ cup plain (all purpose) flour
2 eggs, beaten
250 g / 9 oz / 1 cup breadcrumbs
vegetable oil
salt and pepper

- Open the chicken thighs out like a book.
- Place a piece of ham on top, then cheese and fold over and press the edges together to seal. Secure with cocktail sticks.
- Place the flour, eggs and breadcrumbs on separate plates. Season the flour. Dip each chicken breast into the flour, eggs then breadcrumbs, coating thoroughly each time.
- Heat the oil in a thin layer in the base of a pan then add 2 chicken breasts and cook, turning regularly for about 20 minutes until cooked through.
- Keep warm in a low oven while you cook the remaining chicken. Serve hot.

385

SERVES 4

Basil and Lemon Chicken with Ratatouille

- Marinate the chicken with 2 tbsp oil, lemon zest and a little juice and the basil for 30 minutes.
- Meanwhile heat the remaining oil in a pan and cook the onions.
- Add the aubergines and cook for 2 minutes, then add the garlic and cook for 2 minutes, then add the courgettes and peppers and cook for 5 minutes.
- Crush the coriander seeds and add them to the pan, with the tomatoes. Leave to simmer for at least 30 minutes over a very low heat, stirring occasionally, until the vegetables are very soft. Season and sprinkle over the basil.
- Meanwhile heat a griddle or frying pan and cook the chicken for 6 minutes each side until golden and cooked through. Season and squeeze over a little more lemon juice.
- Serve the chicken with the ratatouille.

PREPARATION TIME 10 MINUTES

COOKING TIME 45 MINUTES

INGREDIENTS

4 chicken breasts
½ lemon, juiced and zested
½ bunch basil
6 tbsp olive oil
2 onions, peeled and finely sliced
2 aubergines (eggplant), diced
2 garlic cloves, finely chopped
3 courgettes (zucchini), diced
3 red peppers, seeded and sliced
400 g / 14 oz / 1 ½ cups canned tomatoes
1 tsp coriander (cilantro) seeds

Pineapple Chicken Colombo

386

SERVES 4

PREPARATION TIME 15 MINUTES

COOKING TIME 30 MINUTES

INGREDIENTS

1 tbsp vegetable oil
4 chicken thighs, skinned, deboned and cubed
salt and pepper
1 onion, peeled and chopped
3 cloves of garlic, crushed
2 tbsp curry powder

6 sprigs thyme leaves
1 tsp ground allspice
½ tsp ground cinnamon
2 bay leaves
1–2 Scotch Bonnet chillies (chilies)
500 ml / 1 pint / 2 cups chicken stock
400 g / 14 oz / 1 ½ cups chopped tomatoes
200 g / 7 oz / ¾ cup pineapple, chopped
cooked white rice to serve

- Heat the oil and sear the chicken on all sides until golden. Remove with a slotted spoon and set aside.
- Add the onion and cook until softened, then add the garlic, spices and herbs and cook for 2 minutes.
- Add the chillies, stock and tomatoes and bring to a simmer. Add the chicken back to the pan, reduce the heat, cover with a lid and cook for 20 minutes until the chicken is cooked.
- Remove the chillies, adjust the seasoning and add the pineapple to heat through.
- Serve with white rice.

Chicken with Roast Vegetables

387

SERVES 4

PREPARATION TIME 10 MINUTES

COOKING TIME 25–40 MINUTES

INGREDIENTS

4 chicken breasts or legs, skin on
2 courgettes (zucchini), thickly sliced
2 red peppers, deseeded and roughly chopped

1 onion, peeled and thickly sliced
4 cloves of garlic, whole
8 cherry tomatoes
60 ml / 2 fl. oz / ¼ cup olive oil
1 bunch basil leaves
salt and pepper

- Preheat the oven to 200°C (180°C fan) / 400F / gas 6.
- Arrange the chicken and vegetables in a roasting tin and drizzle over the oil. Toss to coat. Season well and roast for 25 minutes or until all is cooked through and tender. If using legs, they will take another 10 minutes.
- If the vegetables are still a little pallid-looking, remove the chicken and keep warm and return the tin to the oven for 10 minutes until they start to char appetisingly.
- Serve topped with torn basil.

SPECIAL & SPICY

Chicken Tikka

PREPARATION TIME 20 MINUTES

COOKING TIME 30–35 MINUTES

INGREDIENTS

4 chicken breasts, skinned and chopped
3 tbsp plain yoghurt
2 tbsp tandoori paste
2 tbsp vegetable oil
1 onion, peeled and finely sliced
2 cloves of garlic, finely sliced
knob of ginger, finely sliced
1 cinnamon stick
4 cardamom pods, lightly crushed
1 tsp ground cumin
1 tsp ground coriander (cilantro)
½ tsp turmeric, 2 tsp paprika
400 g / 14 oz / 1 ½ cup tomatoes
100 ml / 3 ½ fl. oz / ½ cup chicken stock
½ lemon, juiced
salt and pepper
250 g / 9 oz / 1 cup basmati rice
500 ml / 1 pint / 2 cups water

- Marinate the chicken for at least 1 hour in the yoghurt and tandoori paste.
- Heat the oil in a pan and fry the onion until golden. Add the garlic, ginger and spices and fry for 2–3 minutes.
- Add the chicken, shaking off any excess marinade, and sauté over high heat until patchily golden, then add the tomatoes and stock and simmer for 20 minutes.
- Once thickened, stir in the remaining marinade and heat through but do not allow to boil.
- Tip the rice into a pan with the water and cook covered with a lid for 10 minutes. Remove from the heat and leave covered for 5 minutes.
- Season the tikka with lemon juice and salt and pepper and serve with rice.

Minted Chicken Tikka

389

- Stir fresh mint leaves through the tikka once cooked for a refreshing kick.

Moroccan Chicken Couscous

PREPARATION TIME 10 MINUTES

COOKING TIME 55 MINUTES

INGREDIENTS

2 tbsp olive oil
1 onion, peeled and finely sliced
2 cloves of garlic, finely sliced
small knob fresh ginger
4 chicken drumsticks, skinned
2 carrots, peeled and chopped
1 tsp ras-el-hanout spice mix
2 cinnamon sticks
1 tsp ground cumin
1 large pinch dried chilli (chili) flakes
400 g / 14 oz / 1 ½ cups canned chickpeas, drained
400 ml / 14 fl. oz / 1 ½ cups chicken stock
200 g / 7 oz / ¾ cup prunes
1 lemon, juiced
sprigs of mint
salt and pepper
couscous to serve

- Heat the oil in a large pan and cook the onions.
- Peel and slice the ginger. Add the garlic and ginger to the pan and cook for a few minutes, then remove all from the pan with a slotted spoon.
- Increase the heat and brown the chicken drumsticks on all sides, then tip the onions back into the pan with the carrots and sprinkle over the spices.
- Pour over the stock, add the chickpeas and prunes and season, lower the heat and cook gently for about 45 minutes or until the sauce has thickened and the chicken is cooked. Stir in the lemon juice and mint.
- Spoon the couscous onto a large serving platter, then spoon the stew on top and serve.

Herby Chicken Couscous

391

- Add chopped fresh flat-leaf parsley, coriander (cilantro) and basil to the couscous.

392
SERVES 2–3

Stir-fried Sesame Chicken

- Heat the oil in a wok and stir fry the chicken until golden. Remove with a slotted spoon and set aside.
- Add the onion, garlic and ginger and fry quickly until golden then return the chicken to the pan with the vegetables. Cook for a few minutes until tender.
- Add the sauces and bubble up.
- Sprinkle in the sesame seeds and serve immediately.

PREPARATION TIME 15 MINUTES

COOKING TIME 15–20 MINUTES

INGREDIENTS

2 tbsp vegetable oil
350 g / 12 oz / 1 ½ cups chicken thigh meat, diced
1 onion, peeled and finely sliced
2 cloves of garlic, finely sliced
1 tsp fresh ginger, grated
100 g / 3 ½ oz / ½ cup beansprouts
1 yellow pepper, deseeded and finely sliced
1 courgette (zucchini), cut into thin batons
2 carrots, peeled and cut into thin batons
2 tbsp soy sauce
2 tbsp oyster sauce
1 tbsp Chinese rice wine or mirin
2 tbsp sesame seeds

Stir-fry with Palm Hearts

393

- Canned palm hearts, widely available, make an interesting addition to the stir fry added at the last minute.

394
SERVES 4

Chicken, Lemon and Olive Tagine

- Heat the oil in a large pan and cook the onions until golden and tender.
- Add the garlic and cook for a few minutes, then remove all from the pan with a slotted spoon.
- Increase the heat and brown the chicken on all sides, then tip the onions back into the pan and sprinkle over the spices. Add the lemons.
- Pour over the stock and season, lower the heat and cook gently for about 45 minutes or until the sauce has thickened and the chicken is cooked.
- Add the olives to warm through, adjust the seasoning and sprinkle with parsley.

PREPARATION TIME 15 MINUTES

COOKING TIME 1 HOUR

INGREDIENTS

2 tbsp olive oil
1 onion, peeled and thickly sliced
2 cloves of garlic, finely sliced
4 chicken legs, skinned
1 tsp ras-el-hanout spice mix
1 tsp ground coriander (cilantro) seeds
1 tsp ground cumin
4 preserved lemons, chopped
1 lemon, chopped
400 ml / 14 fl. oz / 1 ½ cups chicken stock
4 tbsp black olives
½ bunch parsley, chopped
salt and pepper

Chicken Chorizo Tagine

395

- Add chunky slices of chorizo sausage with the onions for colour and spice.

396

SERVES 4

Indian-marinated Chicken

PREPARATION TIME 10 MINUTES

COOKING TIME 15 MINUTES

INGREDIENTS

4 chicken breasts, skinned and cubed
1 red chilli (chili), finely chopped, deseeded if preferred
½ bunch coriander (cilantro) leaves
½ tsp ground turmeric
½ tsp ground coriander (cilantro)
½ tsp ground cumin
½ lemon, juiced
vegetable oil
salt and pepper
basmati rice, cooked, to serve

- Whiz the chilli, coriander and spices in a food processor with lemon juice and enough vegetable oil to make a paste.
- Toss the chicken in the paste and leave to marinate for up to 1 hour in the refrigerator.
- Heat a frying pan with a little oil then wipe off any excess marinade and cook the chicken until golden and sizzling.
- Scrape in any remaining marinade with a little water to make a sauce.
- Serve hot with the basmati rice alongside.

Spiced Chicken with Mustard Seeds

397

- ½ tsp mustard seeds with the spice paste add a strong authentic flavour to the marinade.

398

SERVES 4

Chicken Creole

PREPARATION TIME 15 MINUTES

COOKING TIME 30 MINUTES

INGREDIENTS

2 tbsp olive oil
1 onion, peeled and chopped
1 green pepper, seeded and chopped
1 stick celery, finely chopped
2 cloves of garlic, finely chopped
1 cm (½ in) piece fresh ginger, finely chopped
1 tbsp flour
4 chicken breasts, skinned, cubed
1 tsp paprika
½ tsp Cayenne pepper
400 g / 14 oz / 1 ½ cups chopped tomatoes
100 ml / 3 ½ fl. oz / ½ cup chicken stock
1 bay leaf
salt and pepper
2 mangos, peeled, stoned and cubed
½ lime, juiced
basmati rice, cooked

- Heat the oil in a large pan and sauté the onion, peppers and celery until softened.
- Add the garlic, ginger and flour and cook out for a few seconds, then add the chicken and brown.
- Sprinkle over the spices, then pour in tomatoes and stock. Add the bay leaf and season, then simmer for about 20 minutes over a low heat until the sauce has thickened and the chicken is cooked.
- Serve with the mango tossed with lime juice and the rice alongside.

Chicken Creole with Pistachios

399

- Try using 2 tbsp ground pistachios in the sauce to thicken.

400

SERVES 4

Indian Chicken Curry

Fruity Indian Chicken Curry

401

- Add a couple of handfuls of dried apricots to the sauce to add sweetness and richness.

Creamy Indian Curry

402

- Add 100 ml / 3 ½ fl. oz / ½ cup plain yoghurt at the end of cooking off the heat.

PREPARATION TIME 15 MINUTES

COOKING TIME 40 MINUTES

INGREDIENTS

2 tbsp vegetable oil
4 chicken legs
1 onion, peeled and finely sliced
2 cloves of garlic, finely sliced
1cm piece fresh ginger, grated
1 green chilli (chili), finely chopped
1 tbsp tomato puree
1 tbsp ground coriander (cilantro)
1 tbsp ground cumin
1 tsp turmeric
1 tsp paprika
½ tsp ground cinnamon
400 g / 14 oz / 1 ½ cups canned chopped tomatoes
200 ml / 7 fl. oz / ¾ cup chicken stock
salt and pepper
naan breads and grated coconut, to serve

- Heat the oil in a large pan and sear the chicken on all sides until golden. Remove from the pan and set aside.
- Add the onion, garlic and ginger to the pan and cook until golden. Add the chilli, tomato puree and spices and cook out for 2 minutes.
- Add the chicken back to the pan, then cover with tomatoes and stock.
- Bring to the boil, reduce the heat and simmer very gently for at least 30 minutes until the chicken is cooked through and the sauce has thickened.
- Season well and serve with naan bread and a sprinkling of grated coconut.

403

SERVES 4

Chicken, Chestnut, Prune and Fig Tagine

PREPARATION TIME 10 MINUTES

COOKING TIME 55 MINUTES

INGREDIENTS

2 tbsp olive oil
1 onion, peeled and finely sliced
2 cloves of garlic, finely sliced
small knob fresh ginger, peeled and grated
4 chicken thighs
1 tsp ras-el-hanout spice mix
1 tsp ground cumin
1 tsp ground cinnamon
1 large pinch dried chilli (chili) flakes
400 ml / 14 fl. oz / 1 ½ cups chicken stock
200 g / 7 oz / ¾ cup prunes
150 g / 5 oz / ⅔ cup dried figs
100 g / 3 ½ oz / ½ cup vacuum packed cooked chestnuts
1 orange, juiced
salt and pepper

- Heat the oil in a large pan and cook the onions until golden and tender.
- Add the garlic and ginger and cook for a few minutes, then remove all from the pan with a slotted spoon.
- Increase the heat and brown the chicken thighs on all sides, then tip the onions back into the pan and sprinkle over the spices.
- Pour over the stock, add the prunes, figs and chestnuts and season, lower the heat and cook gently for about 45 minutes or until the sauce has thickened and the chicken is cooked. Stir in the orange juice and heat through.
- Serve with cous cous.

Chicken and Date Tagine

404

- Replace the prunes with dates.

405

SERVES 4

Chilli Lemon Chicken

PREPARATION TIME 10 MINUTES

COOKING TIME 25–30 MINUTES

INGREDIENTS

4 chicken breasts, skinned
1 pinch saffron
1 tbsp olive oil
1 lemon, juiced and zested
1 red chilli (chili), finely chopped
spring onions (scallions)
black olives
salt and pepper
lemon wedges, to serve

- Place the chicken in a pan and pour in enough boiling water to cover. Add the saffron and poach very gently for about 15–20 minutes until cooked through.
- Heat the oil in a pan and add the chilli, then add the chicken and fry for a couple of minutes each side until lightly golden. Squeeze over the lemon juice off the heat and sprinkle with lemon zest.
- Serve with the spring onions, lemon wedges and olives, seasoned with salt, pepper and a little more lemon juice.

Chilli Orange Chicken

406

- Replace the lemon with orange.

407
SERVES 4

Chicken with Chorizo and Tomatoes

- Preheat the oven to 200°C (180°C fan) / 400F / gas 6.
- Place the chorizo, carrot, onion, pepper and tomatoes in a roasting tin. Place the chicken on top and drizzle over the oil.
- Roast in the oven for 30–40 minutes or until the chicken is cooked through, adding a splash of water or white wine if it looks a little dry after 20 minutes.
- Serve sprinkled with coriander.

PREPARATION TIME 10 MINUTES

COOKING TIME 40 MINUTES

INGREDIENTS

4 tbsp olive oil
4 chicken drumsticks, skin on
75 g / 2 ½ oz / ⅓ cup cooking chorizo sausage, sliced
1 carrot, peeled and diced
1 red onion, peeled and thinly sliced
1 yellow pepper, deseeded and diced
8 tomatoes, quartered
salt and pepper
1 tbsp coriander (cilantro) leaves

Chicken with Potatoes, Chorizo and Tomatoes
408

- Adding quartered waxy potatoes to the oven dish makes this a more substantial supper.

409
SERVES 4

Chicken and Seafood Stew

- First cook the mussels: Place in a large pan with a splash of water or white wine and steam with a lid on until all the mussels have opened. Discard any that remain closed and carefully drain off and reserve the mussel liquor, discarding any grit at the bottom.
- In a large pan sweat the onion, celery, carrot and garlic in the oil until softened, then increase the heat and cook the chicken until golden on all sides. Remove with a slotted spoon.
- Add the mussel liquor, tomatoes, stock, saffron, bay leaf and thyme and simmer for 15–20 minutes until the flavour has intensified.
- Add the fish, prawns, peas and chicken, simmer until cooked for about 10 minutes.
- Add the mussels and adjust the seasoning. Serve with bread.

Seafood and Chicken Stew
410

- Try adding half clams, half mussels for a more intense flavour.

PREPARATION TIME 15 MINUTES

COOKING TIME 50 MINUTES

INGREDIENTS

400 g / 14 oz / 1 ½ cups mussels, cleaned and debearded
2 tbsp olive oil
1 onion, peeled and finely sliced
1 stick celery, finely chopped
1 carrot, peeled and finely sliced
2 cloves of garlic, finely sliced
2 chicken thighs, deboned and cubed
200 g / 7 oz / ¾ cup firm white fish, cut into chunks, such as haddock
200 g / 7 oz / ¾ cup shell-on king prawns, raw
400 g / 14 oz / 1 ½ cups chopped tomatoes
500 ml / 1 pint / 2 cups chicken or fish stock
1 pinch saffron
1 bay leaf
1 sprig thyme
salt and pepper
100 g / 3 ½ oz / ½ cup peas

411

SERVES 4

Chicken Fricassee

Chicken Fricassee with Rice

 412

- Serve on a bed of boiled rice.

Fricassee Sandwiches

 413

- Use the leftovers in packed lunch sandwiches.

PREPARATION TIME 10 MINUTES

COOKING TIME 45–50 MINUTES

INGREDIENTS

2 tbsp olive oil
4 chicken drumsticks or thighs
1 onion, peeled and finely sliced
2 cloves of garlic, finely sliced
2 red peppers, deseeded and finely sliced
1 bulb fennel, cored and thickly sliced
2 tomatoes, roughly chopped
4 sprigs thyme
200 ml / 7 fl. oz / ¾ cup white wine
salt and pepper

- Heat the oil in a deep sided pan and fry the chicken on all sides until golden.
- Add the onion and garlic and continue to cook until deep gold and sweet.
- Add the peppers, fennel and tomatoes and cook for a few minutes, then add the thyme and wine, season and cover with a lid.
- Cook over a low heat for 20–25 minutes until the chicken is cooked through.
- Serve with crusty bread

414

SERVES 4

Tandoori-style Chicken

- Prepare the tandoori marinade by mixing together all the ingredients for the marinade in a mixing bowl. Add the chicken, mix well, then cover and chill for at least 1 hour.
- Scrape off any excess marinade and add to a hot wok. When sizzling, add the tomatoes and chicken stock and simmer for 10 minutes. Set aside and keep warm.
- Grill or roast the drumsticks until golden and sticky, then add to the sauce and simmer for 5 minutes to cook through completely.
- Serve the tandoori chicken, sprinkled with coriander.

Tandoori Yoghurt Chicken Skewers

415

- Use cubed chicken in the marinade and grill on skewers for a BBQ version.

PREPARATION TIME
25–30 MINUTES

COOKING TIME 30 MINUTES

INGREDIENTS

8 chicken drumsticks
400 g / 14 oz / 1 ½ cups chopped tomatoes
200 ml / 7 fl. oz / ¾ cup chicken stock
fresh coriander (cilantro) leaves

FOR THE MARINADE
300 ml/10 fl. oz/1 ¼ cups plain yoghurt
1 tsp ground cumin
1 tsp ground coriander (cilantro)
1 tsp garam masala
1 tsp ground cinnamon
1 ½ tsp tandoori chilli (chili) powder
1 tsp caster (superfine) sugar
1 clove garlic, minced
salt and pepper

416

SERVES 4–6

Chicken with Truffles and Sage Butter

- Preheat oven to 220°C (200°C fan) / 425F / gas 7.
- Push the handle of a wooden spoon between the skin and flesh of the chicken breast to create a pocket. Mix the soft butter with seasoning and truffles and push into the pockets to cover the breasts.
- Roast the chicken in the oven for 20 minutes, reduce the heat to 200°C (180°C fan) / 400F / gas 6 and roast for a further hour. Set aside to rest for 15 minutes.
- Meanwhile, heat the remaining butter and olive oil in a pan and sauté the potatoes whole until golden and tender for about 25 minutes.
- Transfer the chicken to a carving board and set the pan full of juices on the hob. Simmer and add the sage leaves and lemon juice, deglazing with a wooden spoon. Adjust the seasoning.
- Carve the chicken and serve with the potatoes, spooning over the truffled sage juices.

Chicken with Herb Butter Stuffing

417

- If your budget doesn't run to truffles, use thyme leaves or basil for the butter stuffing.

PREPARATION TIME 10 MINUTES

COOKING TIME
1 HOUR 30 MINUTES

INGREDIENTS

1 x ready-to-roast chicken
60 g / 2 oz / ¼ cup butter, softened
1 truffle, sliced
salt and pepper
1 kg / 2 lb / 4 ¼ cups new potatoes
30 g / 1 oz butter
olive oil
½ bunch sage leaves
½ lemon, juiced

Green Peppercorn Chicken and Rice

418

SERVES 4

PREPARATION TIME 10 MINUTES

COOKING TIME 15 MINUTES

INGREDIENTS

4 chicken breasts, skinned
4 tbsp bottled green peppercorns
2 tbsp olive oil
250 g / 9 oz / 1 cup basmati rice
500 ml / 1 pint / 2 cups water infused
with pinch saffron
salt
basil, to garnish

- Lightly crush half the peppercorns with the back of a knife and marinate with the chicken for 1 hour.
- Griddle the chicken over medium heat until golden on both sides and cooked through.
- Tip the rice into a pan with the water and cook covered with a lid for 10 minutes. Remove from the heat and leave covered for 5 minutes.
- Serve the chicken sliced with the remaining peppercorns scattered over for heat on top of the rice.

Popping Peppercorn Chicken
 419

- For real colour, use a mixture of pink, green, black and white peppercorns.

Chicken, Almond and Prune Tagine

420

SERVES 4

PREPARATION TIME 10 MINUTES

COOKING TIME 55 MINUTES

INGREDIENTS

2 tbsp olive oil
1 onion, peeled and finely sliced
2 cloves of garlic, finely sliced
small knob fresh ginger, peeled
and grated
4 chicken drumsticks, skinned
2 sweet potatoes, peeled and
roughly chopped
1 tsp ras-el-hanout spice mix
2 cinnamon sticks
1 tsp ground cumin
1 large pinch dried chilli (chili)
flakes
400 ml / 14 fl. oz / 1 ½ cups
chicken stock
200 g / 7 oz / ¾ cup prunes
60 g / 2 oz / ½ cup flaked (slivered)
almonds
1 lemon, juiced
salt and pepper

- Heat the oil in a large pan and cook the onions until golden and tender.
- Add the garlic and ginger and cook for a few minutes, then remove all from the pan with a slotted spoon.
- Increase the heat and brown the chicken drumsticks on all sides, then tip the onions back into the pan with the sweet potato and sprinkle over the spices.
- Pour over the stock, add the prunes and season, lower the heat and cook gently for about 45 minutes or until the sauce has thickened and the chicken is cooked. Stir in the almonds and lemon juice and heat through.
- Serve with cous cous.

Butternut Squash Tagine
 421

- Use butternut squash instead of sweet potato for a similar sweetness but firmer texture.

SERVES 4 422

Peruvian Spicy Chicken

- Poach the chicken in the stock for about 10 minutes, or until just cooked. Remove and reserve 500 ml stock. Cut the chicken into bite-sized pieces.
- Soak the bread in the milk.
- Place the peppers and chilli in a food processor with a little vegetable oil and purée until smooth.
- Heat the olive oil in a pan and cook the onions and garlic until golden, then add the pepper puree and cook until all is soft.
- Whiz the bread/milk until smooth with the walnuts and cheese then add the pepper mixture and combine well.
- Return to the pan, add the reserved chicken stock then add the chicken and heat gently until hot.
- Serve with cooked rice.

PREPARATION TIME 30 MINUTES

COOKING TIME 20 MINUTES

INGREDIENTS

750 g / 1 ½ lb / 3 cups chicken breasts, skinned
1 l / 2 ¼ pints / 4 ¼ cups chicken stock
4 slices white bread
200 ml / 7 fl. oz / 1 ¼ cups milk
3 yellow peppers, deseeded and chopped
1 red chilli (chili), deseeded and chopped
vegetable oil
2 tbsp olive oil
1 onion, peeled and finely sliced
2 cloves of garlic, crushed
3 tbsp walnuts, finely chopped
3 tbsp Parmesan cheese, grated

Spicy Peruvian Chicken with Almonds 423

- Almonds would thicken the sauce as well as walnuts without being as strong in flavour.

SERVES 2 424

Timbale of Vegetables with Chicken

- Preheat the oven to 200°C (180°C fan) / 400F / gas 6.
- Drizzle the chicken with oil, season and roast in the oven for 20 minutes. Leave to rest.
- Meanwhile cut each of the vegetables, except the peas into equal-sized tiny dice.
- Blanch the vegetables separately in boiling salted water for 1 minute, scooping them out with a slotted spoon and refreshing immediately in iced water to retain the colour and stop the cooking.
- Once the vegetables have cooled, dry on kitchen paper. Mix each of the vegetables with a little mayonnaise, just enough to bind and season.
- Set a ring mould on the plate, then layer in the vegetables one at a time. Remove the mould. Repeat.
- Thinly slice the chicken and carefully sit equal slices on top of the timbales. Top with any remaining mayonnaise and serve.

PREPARATION TIME 25 MINUTES

COOKING TIME 20 MINUTES

INGREDIENTS

1 chicken breast, skin on
1 tbsp olive oil
salt and pepper
2 carrots, peeled
200 g / 7 oz / ¾ cup green beans, topped and tailed
150 g / 5 oz / ⅔ cup peas
200 g / 7 oz / ¾ cup baby turnips, peeled and trimmed
100 g / 3 ½ oz / ½ cup mayonnaise

Timbale of Vegetables with Chicken and Rice 425

- Serve on a bed of white boiled rice.

SERVES 4

Caramel Ginger Chicken

PREPARATION TIME 15 MINUTES

COOKING TIME 55 MINUTES

INGREDIENTS

2 tbsp vegetable oil
4 shallots, finely chopped
2 cloves of garlic, finely chopped
5 cm (2 in) piece ginger, peeled and
cut into thin batons
1 lemon, juiced and zested
150 g / 5 oz / ⅔ cup granulated sugar
175 ml / 6 fl. oz / ¾ cup water
2 tbsp soy sauce
8 chicken drumsticks
salt and pepper
300 g / 10 oz / 1 ¼ cups white
rice, cooked according to packet
instructions

- Preheat the oven to 180°C (160°C fan) / 350F / gas 4.
- Heat half the oil in a pan and gently sweat the shallots and garlic. Add the ginger and cook for 2 minutes, then add the remaining ingredients, apart from the chicken and rice, and simmer until thick and syrupy.
- In another pan, sear the chicken in the remaining oil until golden on all sides, then place in a foil-lined roasting tin. Tip the sauce over the chicken, coat thoroughly and roast for about 30–40 minutes until dark, sticky and cooked through.
- Serve with the cooked rice.

Ginger Chicken with Crunchy Vegetables

427

- Souse shredded carrot and courgette in 1 tbsp salt, 2 tbsp vinegar and 1 tsp sugar, then drain and serve alongside.

428

SERVES 4

Tarragon Mustard Chicken

PREPARATION TIME 5 MINUTES
+ MARINATING TIME

COOKING TIME 30 MINUTES

INGREDIENTS

2 tbsp grain mustard
1 tbsp Dijon mustard
1 bunch tarragon
2–3 tbsp olive oil
salt and pepper
4 chicken thighs
½ lemon, juiced

- Preheat the oven to 200°C (180°C fan) / 400F / gas 6.
- Mix together the mustards, half the bunch of tarragon, chopped, oil and seasoning and use to coat the chicken. Leave to marinate for 30 minutes.
- Roast in a foil-lined tin for 30 minutes, until cooked through.
- Serve hot or cold sprinkled with the remaining tarragon and a squeeze of lemon juice.

Tarragon Mustard and Yoghurt Chicken

429

- Make a milder version by adding 2 tbsp yoghurt to the marinade.

430

SERVES 2

Paprika Chicken with Sautéed Vegetables

Creamy Paprika Chicken

 431

- Stir in 150 ml / 5 fl. oz / ⅔ cup sour cream for a quick goulash-style sauté.

Slow-cooked Casserole

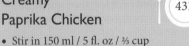 432

- Use chicken legs and 400 ml / 14 fl. oz / 1 ½ cups stock and slow cook in the oven for a winter dish.

PREPARATION TIME 10 MINUTES

COOKING TIME 10 MINUTES

INGREDIENTS

2 tbsp olive oil
2 chicken breasts, skinned and sliced
2 tsp smoked paprika
salt and pepper
100 g / 3 ½ oz / ½ cup chestnut mushrooms, sliced
100 g / 3 ½ oz / ½ cup mange tout
½ lemon, juiced

- Heat the oil in a pan and add the chicken and paprika. Sauté until golden, then add the mushrooms and seasoning and cook until the mushrooms are tender.

- Steam the mange tout over simmering water for 2 minutes, then add to the pan with lemon juice and a splash of water.

- Serve hot.

433
SERVES 4

Chicken Tagine with Sumac and Olives

PREPARATION TIME 15 MINUTES

COOKING TIME 55 MINUTES

....

INGREDIENTS

2 tbsp olive oil
1 onion, peeled and thickly sliced
2 red peppers, deseeded and sliced
2 cloves of garlic, finely sliced
4 chicken legs, skinned
1 tbsp ground sumac
1 tsp ras-el-hanout spice mix
1 tsp ground coriander (cilantro) seeds
1 tsp ground cumin
4 preserved lemons, chopped
400 ml / 14 fl. oz / 1 ½ cups chicken stock
2 tbsp green olives
½ bunch parsley or coriander (cilantro), chopped
salt and pepper

- Heat the oil in a large pan and cook the onions and peppers until golden and tender.
- Add the garlic and cook for a few minutes, then remove all from the pan with a slotted spoon.
- Roll the chicken in the sumac making sure it's thoroughly coated.
- Increase the heat and brown the chicken on all sides, then tip the onions back into the pan and sprinkle over the spices and preserved lemons.
- Pour over the stock and season, lower the heat and cook gently for about 45 minutes or until the sauce has thickened and the chicken is cooked.
- Add the olives to warm through, adjust the seasoning and sprinkle with herbs.

434
SERVES 4

Chinese Chicken and Vegetables with Rice

PREPARATION TIME 30 MINUTES

COOKING TIME 20 MINUTES

....

INGREDIENTS

2 tbsp vegetable oil
1 tsp sesame oil
4 chicken breasts, skinned and sliced
2 carrots, peeled and sliced
knob of fresh ginger, peeled and grated
2 tsp Szechuan peppercorns, roughly crushed
1 tsp black peppercorns, roughly crushed
100 ml / 3 ½ fl oz / ½ cup chicken stock
1–2 tsp sugar
soy sauce
1 tsp cornflour (cornstarch)
handful cooked peas

FOR THE RICE
1 tbsp vegetable oil
550 g / 1 lb / 2 cups cooked white rice
1 onion, peeled and finely chopped
1 garlic clove, peeled and crushed

- Heat the oils in a wok until smoking, then add the chicken and carrots and stir fry over a high heat until the chicken turns white.
- Remove the chicken from the pan and set aside. Discard the oil. Add the stock, sugar and soy and bring to a rapid boil.
- Whisk in the cornflour until thickened then return the chicken to the pan with the peppercorns and peas for a few minutes to cook through.
- To make the rice: Heat the oil in a wok until nearly smoking then add the onion and garlic and stir fry briskly for 3 minutes. Add the rice and combine thoroughly. Stir in some soy sauce and combine until everything is heated through.
- Serve the Cantonese rice with the chicken and sprinkle with the peppercorns.

435
SERVES 4

Chicken Curry

- Heat the oil in a pan and sauté the onion for about 15–20 minutes or until golden-brown.
- Add the garlic and ginger and fry for another minute.
- Add the spices and stir well, then add 200 ml / 7 fl oz / ¾ cup water and cook gently for 10 minutes or so.
- Add the chicken to the sauce and top up with 300 ml / ½ pt / 1 ¼ cups water. Cook at a simmer for around 20 minutes until the chicken is tender.
- Stir in the yoghurt and heat through without boiling.
- Season before serving.

PREPARATION TIME 15 MINUTES

COOKING TIME 50 MINUTES

....

INGREDIENTS

3 tbsp vegetable oil
1 onion, peeled and finely sliced
2 cloves of garlic, chopped
1 tsp fresh ginger, grated
1 tsp ground coriander
pinch turmeric
½ tsp ground cumin
½ tsp garam masala, 1 tsp paprika
450 g / 1 lb / 2 cups chicken thigh meat, skinned and diced
100 g / 3 ½ oz / ½ cup plain yoghurt
salt

436
SERVES 4

Chicken Masala

PREPARATION TIME 20 MINUTES + MARINATING TIME

COOKING TIME 30–35 MINUTES

....

INGREDIENTS

4 chicken breasts
3 tbsp plain yoghurt
2 tbsp tandoori paste
2 tbsp vegetable oil
1 onion, 2 cloves of garlic
knob of ginger, cinnamon stick
4 cardamom pods
1 tsp ground cumin

1 tsp ground coriander (cilantro)
½ tsp turmeric, 1 tsp paprika
400 g / 14 oz / 1 ½ cup chopped tomatoes
100 ml / 3 ½ fl. oz / ½ cup chicken stock
½ lemon, juiced
salt and pepper
basil, to garnish

- Skin and chop the chicken, then marinate for at least 1 hour in the yoghurt and tandoori paste.
- Peel and finely slice the onion, garlic and ginger. Lightly crush the cardamom pods.
- Heat the oil in a pan and fry the onion until golden. Add the garlic, ginger and spices and fry for 2–3 minutes.
- Add the chicken, shaking off any excess marinade, and sauté over high heat until almost golden, then add the remaining marinade, chopped tomatoes and stock, and simmer for 20 minutes.
- Season with lemon juice, salt and pepper and sprinkle with chopped basil.

437
SERVES 4–6

Gingerbread and Port Chicken

PREPARATION TIME 20 MINUTES

COOKING TIME 1 HOUR 40 MINUTES

....

INGREDIENTS

1 oven-ready chicken
30 g / 1 oz butter, softened
salt and pepper

thyme sprigs, 1 star anise
8 shallots, peeled
2 cloves of garlic, unpeeled
2 tbsp olive oil
1–2 tsp flour
200 ml / 7 fl. oz / ¾ cup port
400 ml / 14 fl. oz / 1 ½ cups chicken stock
100 g / 3 ½ oz / ½ cup gingerbread

- Preheat oven to 220°C (200°C fan) / 425F / gas 7.
- Rub the chicken all over with the butter, season well and push the thyme inside the cavity. Place in a roasting tin and roast for 20 minutes.
- Turn the heat down to 180°C (160°C fan) / 350F / gas 4 and add the shallots and garlic and roast for another hour or so until the juices run clear. If the shallots are burning, remove them.
- Transfer the chicken to a platter to rest, covered with foil and place the pan on the heat. Add the shallots back into the pan.
- Stir in the flour and cook out for a couple of minutes, then whisk in the port. Simmer until reduced by half, then whisk in the stock and star anise. Leave to simmer for 10–15 minutes.
- Crumble the gingerbread and sprinkle over the chicken and serve with the port sauce.

438

SERVES 4

Chicken with Tarragon Tomato Sauce

Chicken with Herbed Tomato Sauce

439

- Adding sprigs of rosemary and parsley will add extra heft to the herby flavour.

Chicken with Mascarpone Tomato Sauce

440

- Add 2 large tbsp mascarpone for a creamy sauce and toss with pasta.

PREPARATION TIME 10 MINUTES

COOKING TIME 40 MINUTES

....

INGREDIENTS

2 tbsp olive oil
1 onion, peeled and finely sliced
2 cloves of garlic, finely sliced
1 stick celery, finely sliced
4 chicken legs
3 carrots, peeled and cut into short lengths
12 baby turnips, scrubbed
400 ml / 14 fl. oz / 1 ½ cups passata
300 ml / 10 fl. oz / 1 ¼ cups chicken stock
salt and pepper
2 large sprigs tarragon

- Heat the oil in a large pan and sweat the onion, garlic and celery until softened.
- Add the chicken legs, increase the heat and brown on both sides.
- Add the carrots and turnips, cook for a few minutes, then pour in the passata and stock.
- Simmer for 25–30 minutes or until the chicken is cooked and the vegetables are tender.
- Season and stir through the tarragon before serving.

441

SERVES 4

Chicken Colombo with Bulghur

- Heat the oil and sear the chicken on all sides until golden. Remove with a slotted spoon and set aside.
- Add the onions and carrots and cook until softened, then add the garlic and spices and cook for 2 minutes.
- Add the chillies, cubed potatoes, spring onions and stock and bring to a simmer. Return the chicken to the pan.
- Reduce the heat, cover with a lid and cook for 25 minutes until the potatoes are tender.
- Meanwhile soak the bulghur wheat in the hot stock for 25–30 minutes until tender. Drain off any excess liquid and season.
- Serve the chicken with the bulghur on the side.

PREPARATION TIME 20 MINUTES

COOKING TIME 35 MINUTES

INGREDIENTS

1 tbsp vegetable oil
4 chicken thighs
1 onion, peeled and chopped
2 carrots, peeled and cut into batons
3 cloves of garlic, crushed
2 tbsp curry powder
6 sprigs thyme leaves
1 tsp ground allspice
½ tsp ground cinnamon
2 bay leaves
1-2 Scotch Bonnet chillies (chilies)
8 spring onions, ends trimmed
750 g / 1 ⅓ lb / 3 ¼ cups potatoes, peeled
500 ml / 1 pint / 2 cups chicken stock
FOR THE BULGHUR WHEAT
300 g / 10 oz / 1 ¼ cups bulghur wheat
400 ml / 14 fl. oz / 1 ½ cups chicken stock
salt and pepper

Chicken with Herby Bulghur Wheat

442

- Adding 1 bunch parsley or some mint to the soaked bulghur will add herby freshness.

443

SERVES 4

Chicken Ratatouille

- Preheat the oven to 200°C (180°C fan) / 400F / gas 6.
- Roast the chicken legs in the oven with a little oil and seasoning for 25–30 minutes until cooked. Set aside to rest.
- Meanwhile heat the remaining oil in a pan and cook the onions until deep gold and sweet.
- Add the aubergines and courgettes and cook for 2 minutes, then add the garlic and cook for 2 minutes, then add the peppers and cook for 5 minutes.
- Add the tomatoes, star anise and coriander seeds and leave to simmer for at least 30 minutes over a very low heat, stirring occasionally, until the vegetables are very soft. Season.
- Serve the chicken with the ratatouille and griddled courgette slices and chives.

PREPARATION TIME 10 MINUTES

COOKING TIME 50 MINUTES

INGREDIENTS

4 chicken legs
3 tbsp olive oil
2 onions, peeled and finely sliced
2 aubergines (eggplant), diced
2 garlic cloves, finely chopped
3 red peppers, deseeded and diced
400 g / 14 oz / 1 ½ cups chopped tomatoes
1 star anise
1 tsp coriander (cilantro) seeds, crushed
salt and pepper
3 courgettes (zucchini), diced
2–3 tsp paprika
griddled courgette (zucchini) strips and chives to serve

Chicken Ratatouille Tart

444

- Use a sheet of ready-rolled puff pastry as a base, top with the ratatouille and shredded cooked chicken, then bake in the oven for 20–25 minutes until golden.

445

SERVES 4

Roast Chicken with Spiced Risotto

PREPARATION TIME 10 MINUTES

COOKING TIME 30 MINUTES

....

INGREDIENTS

4 chicken breasts, skin on
4 tbsp olive oil
40 g / 1 oz butter
1 onion, peeled and finely chopped
2 cloves of garlic, finely chopped
1 red chilli (chili), finely diced (optional)
1 cinnamon stick
1 star anise
320 g / 11 oz / 1 ⅓ cups risotto rice
100 ml / 3 ½ fl. oz / ½ cup dry white wine
1 L / 2 ¼ pints / 4 ¼ cups chicken or vegetable stock with pinch saffron threads added
salt and pepper
2 tbsp butter
120 g / 4 oz / ½ cup Parmesan cheese, grated

- Preheat the oven to 200°C (180°C fan) / 400F / gas 6.
- Place the chicken in a roasting tin, drizzle with half the oil, season and roast for 20 minutes.
- Heat the remaining oil and 40 g butter in a large pan and add the onion and garlic. Cook until soft and translucent. Add the rice and stir to coat in the butter and add the spices. Pour in the wine and stir the rice until the wine is absorbed.
- Reduce the heat a little and add the hot stock, a ladleful at a time, stirring fairly continuously.
- Keep stirring in the stock and tasting the rice. After about 15–20 minutes the rice should be soft but with a slight bite.
- Season and remove from the heat. Add the remaining butter and cheese and leave to melt into the risotto. Stir and serve immediately with the chicken.

Chicken with Spiced Couscous

446

- Replace the risotto with couscous.

447

SERVES 4

Thai Chicken Curry with Rice

PREPARATION TIME 10 MINUTES

COOKING TIME 20–25 MINUTES

....

INGREDIENTS

1 tbsp vegetable oil
2 banana shallots, finely chopped
1 tsp fresh ginger, grated
1 stalk lemongrass, finely chopped
1 red pepper, deseeded and finely diced
2–3 tbsp Thai red curry paste
400 ml / 14 fl. oz / 1 ½ cups coconut milk
2 chicken breasts, skinned
1–2 tbsp fish sauce
1–2 tsp sugar
salt and pepper
1 lime, juiced
Thai sticky rice, cooked

- Heat the oil in a wok and fry the shallots, ginger and lemongrass for 2 minutes until softened.
- Add the red pepper and fry for a further 2 minutes.
- Stir in the curry paste and cook out for 2 minutes, stirring. Add the coconut milk and leave to simmer for 10 minutes until thickened.
- Slice the chicken breasts into chunks and add to the curry. Stir in the fish sauce and sugar and simmer until the chicken is cooked.
- Adjust the seasoning and add the lime juice.
- Serve with Thai sticky rice.

Banana Leaf Parcels

448

- If you can source them, wrap a spoonful of rice and curry in a leaf then steam or bake for 10 minutes for people to open at the table.

449

SERVES 2

Chicken Vegetable Noodles

- Cook the noodles in boiling salted water according to packet instructions.
- Heat the oils in a wok and sauté the chicken over high heat until patchily golden.
- Add the carrots, mushrooms, garlic and ginger and stir fry for 2–3 minutes until the mushrooms are tender.
- Add the noodles to the pan with a little cooking water and toss to combine, then add the sauces, stock and spring greens. Heat through until bubbling and the greens are wilted, then serve.

PREPARATION TIME 10 MINUTES

COOKING TIME 10 MINUTES

INGREDIENTS

2 nests of dried ribbon egg noodles
1 tbsp groundnut oil
1 tsp sesame oil
2 chicken thighs, skinned, deboned and chopped
1 carrot, peeled and cut into thin batons
200 g / 7 oz / ¾ cup field or Chinese mushrooms, cleaned
2 cloves of garlic, finely sliced
1 tsp fresh ginger, grated
3–4 tbsp soy sauce
2 tbsp oyster sauce
100 ml / 3 ½ fl. oz / ½ cup chicken stock
150 g / 5 oz / ⅔ cup spring greens, shredded

Chilli Chicken Noodles

450

- Finely chopped red chilli (chili) or 1 tsp chilli oil will add fire.

451

SERVES 4

Stuffed Chicken Breast and Lettuce Flan

- Preheat the oven to 200°C (180°C fan) / 400F / gas 6.
- Season the chicken and lay on a board.
- Heat the butter in a pan and sweat the leeks until soft but not coloured. Leave to cool for 5 minutes, then stir through the cream cheese, seasoning and lemon zest.
- Spoon the leek stuffing down the middle of each chicken breast, roll the meat into a sausage shape and tie with cooking string to secure. Roast in the oven for 30–45 minutes. Leave to rest before carving.
- Meanwhile heat the butter in a pan and sweat the shallots for a few minutes. Stir in the lettuces and season.
- Whisk together the eggs, cream and water and a little salt. Stir the lettuce and shallots into the mixture then pour into a 12-hole greased muffin tin.
- Bake in the oven for 20 minutes until puffed and golden. Serve alongside stuffed chicken breasts.

PREPARATION TIME 15 MINUTES

COOKING TIME 45 MINUTES

INGREDIENTS

4 chicken breasts, beaten out to an even thickness
50 g / 1 ¾ oz / ¼ cup butter
2 leeks, trimmed and finely sliced
200 g / 7 oz / ¾ cup cream cheese
salt and pepper
½ lemon, zested

FOR THE FLANS
30 g / 1 oz butter
2 shallots, finely chopped
2 little gem lettuces, shredded
12 eggs
120 ml / 4 fl. oz / ½ cup double (heavy) cream
120 ml / 4 fl. oz / ½ cup water

Stuffed Chicken with Mushroom Flan

452

- Substitute 200 g / 7 oz / ¾ finely sliced chestnut mushrooms for the lettuces for a more substantial accompaniment.

453

SERVES 4

Chicken and Beef Kebabs

Balsamic Meat Kebabs

454

- Try drizzling the meats with balsamic instead for a sweet sharp flavour.

Surf and Turf

455

- Alternate large prawns with the other ingredients.

PREPARATION TIME 10 MINUTES

COOKING TIME 10 MINUTES

··

INGREDIENTS

4 chicken breasts, skinned and cubed
1 tbsp thyme leaves
1 tbsp olive oil
400 g / 14 oz / 1 ½ cups rump steak, cubed
2 tbsp teriyaki sauce
8–12 cherry tomatoes
1 green pepper, deseeded and roughly chopped
1 red pepper, deseeded and roughly chopped
1 onion, peeled and cut into large chunks
1 lemon, sliced
salt and pepper

- Mix the chicken with thyme, olive oil and seasoning. Mix the steak with teriyaki and pepper.
- Thread onto soaked wooden skewers alternating with the vegetables, tomatoes and lemon slices.
- Griddle or barbecue over high heat - the chicken will take about 10 minutes, the steak much less, if you like it pink.
- Serve hot or warm.

456

SERVES 2–4

Tandoori Chicken

- Heat the oil in a wok and sauté the chicken over high heat until golden.
- Mix together the ingredients for the tandoori sauce in a small pan and heat through very gently without boiling.
- Place a banana leaf in each bowl, spoon chicken into the centre and spoon over the tandoori sauce. Serve with lime wedges.

PREPARATION TIME 10 MINUTES

COOKING TIME 10 MINUTES

INGREDIENTS

4 chicken thighs, skinned, deboned and cubed
1 tbsp groundnut oil
banana leaves
lime wedges

FOR THE SAUCE
1 tsp ground cumin
1 tsp ground coriander (cilantro)
1 tsp garam masala
1 tsp ground cinnamon
1 ½ tsp tandoori chilli (chili) powder
1 tsp caster (superfine) sugar
1 tsp paprika
1 clove of garlic, minced
salt and pepper
200 ml / 7 fl. oz / ¾ cup plain yoghurt

Tandoori Parathas

 457

- Roll the chicken and sauce into ready-made parathas or chapattis for a filling snack.

458

SERVES 4

Chicken, Sweet Potato and Grape Stew

- Heat the oil in a large pan and cook the onions until golden and tender.
- Add the garlic and cook for a few minutes, then remove all from the pan with a slotted spoon.
- Increase the heat and brown the chicken drumsticks on all sides, then tip the onions back into the pan with the sweet potato and sprinkle over the spices.
- Pour over the stock, add the grapes and raisins and season. Lower the heat and cook gently for about 45 minutes or until the sauce has thickened and the chicken is cooked. Stir in the almonds and lemon juice and heat through.
- Serve with cous cous.

PREPARATION TIME 10 MINUTES

COOKING TIME 55 MINUTES

INGREDIENTS

2 tbsp olive oil
1 onion, peeled and finely sliced
2 cloves of garlic, finely sliced
4 chicken drumsticks, skinned
2 sweet potatoes, peeled and roughly chopped
1 tsp ras-el-hanout spice mix
2 cinnamon sticks
1 tsp ground cumin
1 large pinch dried chilli (chili) flakes
400 ml / 14 fl. oz / 1 ½ cups chicken stock
200 g / 7 oz / ¾ cup green grapes, seedless
2 tbsp golden raisins
2 tbsp whole almonds, skinned
1 lemon, juiced
salt and pepper

Grated Courgette Salad

 459

- Grate a courgette (zucchini) into a bowl and mix with lemon juice and toasted black onion seeds and serve alongside.

460

SERVES 4

Grilled Chicken with Paprika

PREPARATION TIME 10 MINUTES

COOKING TIME 50 MINUTES

INGREDIENTS

4 chicken drumsticks, skin on
4 tbsp olive oil
1 tbsp smoked paprika
2 onions, peeled and finely sliced
2 aubergines (eggplant), diced
1 courgette (zucchini), diced
2 garlic cloves, finely chopped
3 red peppers, seeded and cut
into strips
400 g / 14 oz / 1 ½ cups chopped
tomatoes
1 tsp coriander (cilantro) seeds,
crushed
salt and pepper
2 sprigs fresh thyme
½ lemon, juiced

- Preheat the oven to 200°C (180°C fan) / 400F / gas 6.
- Roast the chicken legs in the oven rubbed with half the oil and the paprika and seasoning for 25–30 minutes until cooked. Set aside to rest.
- Meanwhile heat the remaining oil in a pan and cook the onions until deep gold and sweet.
- Add the aubergines and cook for 2 minutes, then add the courgettes and cook for 2 minutes, then add the peppers and garlic and cook for 5 minutes.
- Add the tomatoes, thyme sprigs and coriander seeds and leave to simmer for at least 30 minutes over a very low heat, stirring occasionally, until the vegetables are very soft. Season.
- Squeeze the lemon over the chicken and serve with the ratatouille.

Chilli Chicken with Ratatouille 461

- Spicy chilli (chili) paste or even harissa can be rubbed onto the chicken before roasting.

462

SERVES 2

Chinese Chicken with Noodles

PREPARATION TIME 10 MINUTES

COOKING TIME 25 MINUTES

INGREDIENTS

2 chicken breasts, skinned
500 ml / 1 pint / 2 cups weak
chicken stock
2 nests vermicelli noodles
1 tbsp vegetable oil
1 tbsp sesame oil
1 bunch spring onions (scallions),
finely chopped
1 carrot, peeled and diced
1 courgette (zucchini), diced
1 cm piece ginger, grated
2 cloves of garlic, finely sliced
4 tbsp soy sauce
2 tbsp unsalted peanuts, chopped
strips of mooli (daikon) or cucumber,
to garnish

- Poach the chicken in the stock very gently for about 20 minutes or until cooked through. Set aside to rest, reserving the chicken stock.
- Soak the noodles in the chicken stock according to packet instructions and drain when tender.
- Meanwhile heat the oils in a wok and sauté the carrots, courgettes, spring onions, ginger and garlic over a high heat, then add the noodles and soy sauce.
- Toss well to heat through and serve topped with sliced chicken. Sprinkle with peanuts and mooli or cucumber to garnish.

Chicken Noodle Soup 463

- You could serve this in deep bowls with the reserved chicken stock ladled over piping hot.

464

SERVES 4

Chicken with Chilli Prawns

Chicken with Seafood

465

- Chicken works well with all seafood. Try adding squid rings, mussels or clams for extra fishy flavour.

Chicken Chilli Prawn Pasta

466

- Toss with spaghetti and sprinkle with more parsley.

PREPARATION TIME 5 MINUTES

COOKING TIME 30 MINUTES

INGREDIENTS

80 ml / 2 ½ fl. oz / ⅓ cup olive oil
8 small chicken portions, such as
drumsticks, wings or thighs, skin on
2 cloves of garlic, finely sliced
1 red chilli (chili), finely sliced
16 large prawns (shrimps),
raw and shell on
½ bunch parsley, finely chopped
salt and pepper
½ lemon, juiced

- Heat the oil in a deep-sided pan and brown the chicken on all sides.
- Lower the heat and leave to cook until the juices run clear when pierced with the point of a knife.
- Add the garlic and chilli and cook briefly, then add the prawns and toss until the prawns turn pink and are cooked.
- Sprinkle over parsley and seasoning, then squeeze over the lemon juice and serve in bowls with crusty bread.

467

SERVES 4–6

Chicken with Pineapple and Lime

PREPARATION TIME 10 MINUTES

COOKING TIME 30 MINUTES

INGREDIENTS

1 chicken, jointed
1 tbsp olive oil
1 tbsp honey
1 lime, zested
½ tsp cayenne pepper
salt and pepper
1 pineapple, peeled, cored and
cut into large chunks
1–2 limes, juiced
1 red onion, peeled and finely sliced
cooked rice, to serve

- Coat the chicken with the oil, honey, lime zest and cayenne.
- Cook over a barbecue for 20–30 minutes until golden and cooked through, turning often so the honey does not burn. Season well.
- Meanwhile, thread the pineapple onto skewers and cook alongside the chicken for 5 minutes.
- Serve the cooked chicken with the pineapple chunks, doused in lime juice and sprinkled with red onion, on a bed of rice.

468

SERVES 4

Indian Chicken Soup

PREPARATION TIME 15 MINUTES

COOKING TIME 40–45 MINUTES

INGREDIENTS

2 tbsp groundnut oil
2 onions, peeled and sliced
1 carrot, peeled and sliced
2 cloves of garlic, finely sliced
4 chicken thighs, skinned,
deboned and cubed
1 aubergine (eggplant), finely diced
1 tbsp garam masala
½ tsp black onion seeds
4 curry leaves
2 tbsp tomato puree
400 ml / 14 fl. oz / 1 ½ cups chicken
stock
salt and pepper
chopped coriander (cilantro)
naan bread, to serve

- Heat the oil in a large pan and fry the onions until very dark gold.
- Add the carrot, aubergine and garlic and fry for 2 minutes, then add the chicken and cook until the chicken is patchily golden.
- Add the spices and tomato puree and cook out for 2 minutes, stirring to coat the chicken, then add the stock and leave to simmer for 20 minutes.
- Serve with naan bread and a sprinkling of coriander.

469

SERVES 6

Yassa Chicken

- Marinate the chicken in the lemon juice, onions, seasoning, chilli and a little oil for at least 4 hours.
- Preheat the oven to 200°C (180°C fan) / 400F / gas 6.
- Remove the chicken from the marinade and roast the chicken pieces in the oven for 20 minutes or so until golden.
- Meanwhile cook the onions from the marinade in 1 tbsp oil in a pan until tender, then add the remaining marinade and heat through. Add the habanero, olives, and 100 ml / 3 ½ fl. oz / ¼ cup water and simmer for 10 minutes until slghtly reduced. Remove the habanero.
- Serve the roast chicken pieces on a bed of rice with the onion and olive sauce spooned over.

PREPARATION TIME 5 MINUTES

COOKING TIME 40 MINUTES

INGREDIENTS

2 tbsp lemon juice
2 onions, peeled and finely sliced
salt and pepper
1 green chilli (chili), finely chopped
1 chicken, jointed into 6 pieces
2 tbsp peanut or groundnut oil
1 habanero chilli (chili), pricked with a fork
100 g / 3 ½ oz / ½ cup green olives
cooked white rice, to serve

Chicken with Gratin Dauphinois

470

SERVES 4-6

PREPARATION TIME 20 MINUTES

COOKING TIME 1 ½–2 HOURS

INGREDIENTS

50 g / 1 ¾ oz / ¼ cup butter, softened
1 kg / 2 ¼ lb / 4 ¼ cups floury potatoes, peeled
2 cloves of garlic, crushed

salt and pepper
½ bunch thyme
500 ml / 1 pint / 2 cups double (heavy) cream
FOR THE CHICKEN
1 oven-ready chicken
4 cloves of garlic
4 sprigs of thyme
40 g / 1 oz butter, softened

- Preheat oven to 160°C (140°C fan) / 300F / gas 2.
- Use the softened butter to generously grease a large baking dish.
- Slice the potatoes as thinly as possible.
- Layer the potatoes in the baking dish, seasoning and sprinkling with thyme leaves and garlic as you go.
- Pour the cream over the potatoes – it should come to the top of the potatoes. Push the potatoes down into the cream, place on a baking tray and bake for 1 ½ hours until the potatoes are completely tender.
- Stuff the cavity of the chicken with garlic and thyme, rub the butter over the skin and season. Place in a roasting tin and roast in the oven with the potatoes for 1 ½ hours.
- Remove the potatoes from the oven and leave to settle before serving. Grill the chicken until the skin is crisp and golden.
- Leave the chicken to rest then carve and serve with the potatoes.

Chicken with Vodka and Bulghur

471

SERVES 6

PREPARATION TIME 20 MINUTES

COOKING TIME 40 MINUTES

INGREDIENTS

2 tbsp olive oil
1 chicken, jointed
100 ml / 3 ½ fl. oz / ½ cup vodka
1 onion, peeled and thickly sliced

2 peppers, deseeded and roughly chopped
2 cloves of garlic, finely sliced
300 g / 10 oz / 1 ¼ cups bulghur wheat
400 ml / 14 fl. oz / 1 ½ cups chicken stock
mint leaves
salt and pepper

- Preheat the oven to 180°C (160°C fan) / 350F / gas 4.
- Heat the oil in an oven-proof casserole and brown the chicken on all sides, in batches so as not to overcrowd the pan. Remove from the pan.
- Add the onion, peppers and garlic and cook for 10 minutes until softened, then remove from the pan with a slotted spoon. Deglaze with vodka, scraping with a wooden spoon.
- Return the chicken and vegetables to the pan with the bulghur and stock and simmer. Transfer to the oven and bake for 30–40 minutes until the chicken is cooked through and the bulghur is tender. Check periodically as you may need to add more water if it looks dry.
- Stir through mint leaves and seasoning and serve.

472

SERVES 2

Spicy Beer-roasted Chicken

Quick Chicken Stir-fry

473

- Use chopped chicken and mushrooms and stir fry in a wok, using half the beer and soy to make a quick simple version.

Rice Wine Stir-fry

474

- Use the same amount of rice wine instead of beer for a different flavour.

PREPARATION TIME 10 MINUTES

COOKING TIME 50 MINUTES

INGREDIENTS

2-4 chicken drumsticks
2 tbsp vegetable oil
75 ml / 2 ½ fl. oz / ⅓ cup soy sauce
2 tsp sugar
400 ml / 14 fl. oz / 1 ¾ cups Asian lager
8 large shiitake or field mushrooms
1 onion, peeled
4 tbsp soy sauce
1 green chilli (chili), chopped
juice of ½ lime (optional)
black pepper

- Preheat the oven to 200°C (180°C fan) / 400F / gas 6.
- Place the drumsticks in a roasting tin. Mix together the oil, 4 tbsp soy and the sugar and coat the drumsticks thoroughly. Pour three quarters of the beer into the roasting tin and add the mushrooms and the onion cut into 8 wedges. Roast for 30–40 minutes until the chicken is cooked through and all is sticky and golden.
- Remove the contents from the pan to a plate and place the roasting tin on the heat. Deglaze the pan with the remaining beer and reduce until syrupy with the chilli and the remaining soy. Taste and adjust the seasoning, adding the lime if desired.
- Serve the chicken and mushrooms with the sauce spooned over.

SERVES 4

Chicken and Tarragon Sausage

- Peel and core the apples and cut into chunks. Place in a pan with the sugar, cloves and water and cover with a lid. Cook over a low heat for 10–15 minutes until the apples are very soft. Beat until fairly smooth, remove the cloves and set aside.
- Place the chicken and onion in a food processor and blend, adding a tbsp of cream and combine. Add the remaining cream, blend well, scrape into a bowl, season and add the tarragon. Cover with cling film and chill.
- Cut 4 large squares of cling film and divide the chicken mixture equally between them. Wrap the film tightly around the chicken to form a sausage shape.
- Poach in simmering water for 8-10 minutes.
- Heat the butter and fry the garlic and mushrooms until tender. Season and stir in the parsley.
- Unwrap the sausages and serve with mushrooms and apple sauce.

Chicken Mousse Stuffing

- You could use this mousse as a stuffing for pork, rabbit or even mushrooms as it will cook within the meat you have wrapped it in.

PREPARATION TIME 45 MINUTES

COOKING TIME 20 MINUTES

INGREDIENTS

250 g / 9 oz / 1 cup Bramley apples
250 g / 9 oz / 1 cup Cox apples
1 tbsp sugar (optional, depending on tartness of apples)
2 cloves
2 tbsp water
2 chicken breasts, skinned
1 small onion, peeled and chopped
200 ml / 7 fl. oz / ¾ cup double (heavy) cream
2 tbsp tarragon leaves, chopped
salt and pepper
40 g / 1 oz butter
200 g / 7 oz / ¾ cup chanterelle mushrooms, cleaned
1 clove of garlic, crushed
1 tbsp chopped parsley

SERVES 4

Chicken with Fennel, Olives and Lemons

- Heat the oil in a large casserole and brown the chicken legs on both sides until golden. You may need to cook them 2 at a time. Remove to a plate.
- Add the onion and garlic to the pan and cook gently until softened and gold. Add the fennel and cook for 2 minutes, before adding the cumin, lemons, bay leaf and chicken back to the pan. Cover with the stock, reduce the heat and simmer gently for 30–40 minutes until the chicken has cooked through.
- 5 minutes before the end of cooking, stir in the olives. When cooked, adjust the seasoning carefully, as olives are naturally salty, and serve.

Chicken with Fennel and Rice

- You could add 150 g / 5 oz / ¾ cup rice in with the chicken to cook in the stock to stretch this dish further. You might need a fraction more stock.

PREPARATION TIME 10 MINUTES

COOKING TIME 55 MINUTES

INGREDIENTS

3 tbsp olive oil
4 chicken legs
1 onion, peeled and sliced
2 cloves of garlic, finely sliced
2 fennel bulbs, cored and sliced
1 tsp ground cumin
1 bay leaf
3 preserved lemons, chopped
300 ml / 10 fl. oz / 1 ¼ cups chicken stock
100 g / 3 ½ oz / ½ cup green olives
salt and pepper

479 | SERVES 4

Chicken à la Nage

PREPARATION TIME 15 MINUTES

COOKING TIME 10–15 MINUTES

INGREDIENTS

2 chicken breasts, skinned
1 stick celery, finely sliced
1 leek, trimmed and finely sliced
2 carrots, peeled and cut into matchsticks
2 red peppers, deseeded and finely sliced
8 black peppercorns
1 bay leaf
1 bunch parsley stalks, leaves reserved
400 ml / 14 fl. oz / 1 ½ cups hot chicken stock
½ bunch chives, finely chopped
salt and pepper

- Finely slice the chicken breasts and place in a large pan with the vegetables, peppercorns, bay leaf and parsley stalks. Pour over the stock, simmer and skim off any scum that floats to the surface.
- Poach the chicken and vegetables until just tender, around 10–15 minutes.
- Ladle into deep bowls and stir through the chives and seasoning. Serve hot.

Chicken à la Nage with Thai Flavourings

 480

- Try adding a chopped chilli, 2 tbsp fish sauce and a squeeze of lime for a fresh take on this soup.

481 | SERVES 4-6

Chicken and Sweet Potato Mafé

PREPARATION TIME 20 MINUTES
+ MARINATING TIME

COOKING TIME 45 MINUTES

INGREDIENTS

1 chicken, jointed into 6 pieces
250 g / 9 oz / 1 cup plain yoghurt
250 g / 9 oz / 1 cup tomatoes, chopped
1 cinnamon stick
3 cardamom pods, lightly crushed
4 cloves
6 black peppercorns
1 tsp cumin seeds
2-3 green chillies (chilies), chopped
½ tsp turmeric
1 tsp cayenne pepper (optional)
1 tsp paprika
2 tsp fresh ginger, grated
salt and pepper
3 tbsp vegetable oil
2 onions, peeled and finely sliced
2 red peppers, deseeded and finely sliced
3 sweet potatoes, peeled and diced

- Place the chicken in a large non-reactive bowl.
- Mix together the yoghurt, tomatoes, spices, chillies, ginger and some salt and coat the chicken thoroughly. Refrigerate for 1–2 hours to marinate.
- Heat the oil in a pan and cook the onions gently until golden. Add the peppers and cook for 5–8 minutes until tender.
- Add the chicken and the marinade and cook gently until the chicken is cooked all the way through. You will need to add a little water every now and then to prevent the sauce sticking. It should take about 25–35 minutes.
- Meanwhile steam the sweet potatoes for about 10 minutes until tender.
- Serve the chicken spooned over the sweet potatoes.

Fruity Chicken Curry

 482

- This sauce lends itself well to the addition of fruit such as dried apricots, prunes or even diced apples.

483

SERVES 4

Traditional Paella

Pork, Chicken and Seafood Paella

484

- Add pork to the paella for a meatier dish.

Pepper Paella

485

- Add a mix of coloured peppers to the paella.

PREPARATION TIME 20 MINUTES

COOKING TIME 40 MINUTES

INGREDIENTS

5 tbsp olive oil
1 onion, peeled and finely sliced
2 cloves of garlic, finely chopped
1 celery stick, finely chopped
1 red pepper, seeded and sliced
300 g / 10 oz / 1 ¼ cups paella rice
4 chicken thighs
4–6 cocktail sausages
1 l / 2 ¼ pints / 4 ¼ cups chicken or vegetable stock
pinch saffron threads
1 tsp paprika
4 ripe tomatoes, chopped
12 raw prawns, shell on
8 baby squid, cleaned
4 mussels, cooked
1 lemon
salt and pepper
chopped parsley, to garnish

- Heat the olive oil in a large shallow pan and cook the onion, garlic and celery until softened.
- Add the pepper, cook for a further 5 minutes, then stir in the chicken, sausages and paella rice and coat thoroughly in the oil.
- Stir the saffron into the stock then pour it over the rice. Add the paprika. Simmer uncovered for 15 minutes. Add more stock if it looks dry.
- Add the tomatoes, squid and prawns and cook for a further 8–10 minutes until everything is just cooked through.
- Stir through the lemon juice and parsley, season well and serve topped with mussels.

486

SERVES 4

Saffron Chicken with Sorrel Sauce

PREPARATION TIME 10 MINUTES

COOKING TIME 20 MINUTES

INGREDIENTS

4 chicken breasts
600 ml / 1 pint / 2 ½ cups chicken stock
1 pinch saffron
500 g / 1 lb / 2 cups new potatoes, in their skins
250 g / 9 oz / 1 cup sorrel leaves
1 tbsp butter
120 ml / 4 fl. oz / ½ cup crème fraiche
salt and pepper

- Gently simmer the chicken in stock infused with the saffron for 20 minutes or until cooked.
- Cook the potatoes whole in boiling salted water for 20 minutes until tender to the point of a knife. Drain thoroughly.
- Meanwhile wilt the sorrel in a non-reactive pan with the butter, then stir in the creme fraiche. Transfer to a food processor and blitz until smooth.
- When ready to serve, transfer the sauce back to the pan and reheat gently, correcting the seasoning (if you do this before you are ready, the sauce will turn grey).
- Serve the chicken and potatoes on top of the sauce.

Saffron Rice with Spinach Sauce 487

- If sorrel is hard to get hold of, use the same amount of spinach with a squeeze of lemon juice and a little grated nutmeg.

488

SERVES 4

Tandoori Chicken Drumsticks

PREPARATION TIME 10 MINUTES
+ MARINATING TIME

COOKING TIME 25 MINUTES

INGREDIENTS

8 chicken drumsticks
salad leaves, to serve

FOR THE MARINADE
300 ml /10 fl. oz / 1 ¼ cups plain yoghurt
1 tsp ground cumin
1 tsp ground coriander (cilantro)
1 tsp garam masala
1 tsp ground cinnamon
1 ½ tsp tandoori chilli (chili) powder
1 tsp paprika
1 tsp caster (superfine) sugar
1 clove garlic, minced
salt and pepper

- Prepare the tandoori marinade by mixing together all the ingredients for the marinade in a mixing bowl. Add the chicken, mix well, then cover and chill for at least 1 hour.
- Preheat the oven to 200°C (180°C fan) / 400F / gas 6.
- Tip the chicken and marinade into a foil-lined roasting tin and roast for 25–30 minutes until the chicken is dark gold and cooked through.
- Serve with a fresh salad.

Tandoori Kebabs with Peppers 489

- Use diced chicken and thread onto skewers with green peppers.

490

SERVES 4

Chicken Cooked with Cola

- Put the cola, chilli, peppercorns and fenel seeds in a large saucepan and simmer for 5 minutes.
- Add the chicken breasts and carrots and poach gently for 20 minutes or until the chicken is just cooked.
- Remove from the poaching liquor with a slotted spoon and serve, perhaps with creamy mashed potato.

PREPARATION TIME 5 MINUTES

COOKING TIME 25 MINUTES

INGREDIENTS

1 red chilli (chili)
6 black peppercorns
1 tsp fennel seeds, lightly crushed
500 ml / 1 pint / 2 cups cola
4 chicken breasts, skinless
2 carrots, peeled and cut into thin batons

Chicken with Cherry Cola **491**

- Replace the cola with cherry cola for a sweeter taste.

492

SERVES 4

Chicken and Vegetable Brochettes

- Toss the chicken chunks with quatre epices, oil and seasoning. Leave to marinate for 20 minutes.
- Thread the chicken onto soaked wooden skewers alternating with the peppers, courgette, tomatoes and onion.
- Grill or griddle until the chicken is golden and just cooked through, about 8–10 minutes.
- Serve with lemon juice squeezed over and a little more salt.

PREPARATION TIME 30 MINUTES

COOKING TIME 10 MINUTES

INGREDIENTS

4 chicken breasts, skinned and cut into chunks
1 tbsp quatre epices
4 tbsp olive oil
salt and pepper
1 yellow pepper, deseeded and roughly chopped
1 green pepper, deseeded and roughly chopped
½ courgette (zucchini), thickly sliced
1 red onion, peeled and thickly sliced
4 cherry tomatoes
½ lemon, juiced

Chicken and Prawn Brochettes **493**

- Raw king prawns make a good meaty addition to the kebabs.

494

SERVES 4

Mexican-style Chicken Hash

Chicken Chilli

495

- This is only a few steps away from chilli. Use canned tomatoes, a little sliced chorizo and 1 tsp cocoa powder all simmered for 30 minutes.

Chicken Chilli Tortilla Tower

496

- Layer the mix between warmed tortilla wraps in a tower to serve at the table.

PREPARATION TIME 15 MINUTES

COOKING TIME 30–35 MINUTES

INGREDIENTS

2 tbsp olive oil
1 onion, peeled and chopped
4 chicken thighs, skinned, deboned and chopped
2 red peppers, deseeded and chopped
1 yellow pepper, deseeded and chopped
2 cloves of garlic, finely sliced
400 g / 14 oz / 1 ½ cups red kidney beans or black beans, drained
6 ripe tomatoes, cored and chopped
2 tsp smoked paprika
1 lime, juiced
2–3 dried chillies (chilies), rehydrated
and chopped (or less if you want it milder)
salt and pepper
chopped parsley, to serve

- Heat the oil in a large pan and cook the onion until golden. Add the chicken thighs, increase the heat slightly and cook until patchily golden.

- Add the peppers and fry for 4 minutes or until starting to soften, then add the garlic and cook for another minute.

- Add the beans, tomatoes, paprika, lime juice and chillies and a glass of water and simmer for 10–15 minutes until the chicken is cooked and all is tender.

- Season well and serve hot with parsley and crusty bread.

497

SERVES 4

Chicken Tandoori Escalopes

- Place the chicken breasts between 2 pieces of cling film and bash with a rolling pin until about 1 cm thick.
- Mix together all the spices and oil and coat the chicken thoroughly. Marinate for 4 hours or overnight.
- When ready to cook, heat a little oil in a pan and cook the escalopes in batches until golden and just cooked through, about 2–3 minutes per side.
- Serve with lime wedges, red onion and cooked rice, if desired.

PREPARATION TIME 10 MINUTES
+ MARINATING TIME

COOKING TIME 6–7 MINUTES

··

INGREDIENTS

4 skinless chicken breasts
lime wedges, sliced red onion and cooked rice, to serve

FOR THE MARINADE

2 tbsp groundnut oil
1 tsp ground cumin
1 tsp ground coriander (cilantro)
1 tsp garam masala
1 tsp ground cinnamon
1 ½ tsp tandoori chilli (chili) powder
1 tsp caster (superfine) sugar
1 clove garlic, minced
salt and pepper

Chicken Tandoori Pizza

498

- Cut the marinated chicken into small pieces, add to a traditional pizza and crumble feta over the top before baking.

499

SERVES 2–4

Two Chicken Stews

- Divide the chicken equally so half the pieces will go in each stew and set aside. Add the saffron to the stock for the pea stew.
- Heat the oil in a casserole and sweat the onion and garlic for 5–10 minutes until softened. Increase the heat, add half the chicken pieces and brown on all sides.
- Add the peas, mange tout, almonds, lemon and saffron infused stock and simmer for 30 minutes or until the chicken is cooked through and liquid reduced. Season.
- Repeat the same process for the second stew, adding the potatoes, almonds and the stock and simmering until the chicken is cooked. Season.
- Serve in 2 serving bowls with crusty bread.

PREPARATION TIME 10 MINUTES

COOKING TIME 45 MINUTES

··

INGREDIENTS

1 chicken, jointed into 6 pieces

FOR THE PEA STEW

2 tbsp olive oil
1 onion, peeled and finely sliced
1 clove of garlic, finely sliced
100 g / 3 ½ oz / ½ cup peas
100 g / 3 ½ oz / ½ cup mange tout
60 g / 2 oz / ⅓ cup skinned almonds
½ lemon, sliced
400 ml / 14 fl. oz / 1 ½ cups chicken stock
pinch saffron, salt and pepper

FOR THE SWEET POTATO STEW

2 tbsp olive oil
1 onion, peeled and finely sliced
1 clove of garlic, finely sliced
2 sweet potatoes, peeled and diced
60 g / 2 oz / ⅓ cup skinned almonds
400 ml / 14 fl. oz / 1 ½ cups chicken stock

Chicken Vegetable Stew

500

- This basic process can be followed to make any kind of vegetable chicken stew. Try using celeriac, quartered fennel, broccoli or carrots.

501

SERVES 4

Vietnamese Chicken Curry

PREPARATION TIME 10 MINUTES

COOKING TIME 35–40 MINUTES

INGREDIENTS

1 tbsp groundnut oil
4 chicken thighs, skinned
2 onions, peeled and sliced
1 red chilli (chili), deseeded and finely chopped
3 cloves of garlic, finely chopped
3 stalks lemongrass, bruised
2 tsp ground coriander (cilantro)
1 tsp turmeric
400 ml / 14 fl. oz / 1 ½ cups coconut milk
200 ml / 7 fl. oz / ¾ cup chicken stock
2 tbsp fish sauce
1 tbsp soft dark brown sugar
salt and pepper
1 bunch basil leaves (or Thai holy basil, if you can get it)

- Heat the oil in a wok and brown the chicken thighs on all sides.
- Add the onions, chilli, garlic and lemongrass and cook for 5 minutes until the onions are golden.
- Add the coriander and turmeric, stir to coat, then add the coconut milk and stock, fish sauce, sugar and a little seasoning and simmer for 20–25 minutes until the chicken is cooked through.
- Stir in the basil and serve with cooked rice.

Vietnamese Noodles

502

- Make the recipe the same way with chopped chicken, but only use half the amount of coconut milk and toss with cooked rice noodles.

503

SERVES 4

Chicken Cakes with Chilli Sauce

PREPARATION TIME 15 MINUTES

COOKING TIME 35 MINUTES

INGREDIENTS

500 g / 1 lb / 2 cups chicken, minced
2 onions, peeled and finely chopped
4 cloves of garlic, crushed
½ bunch coriander (cilantro), chopped
salt and pepper
1 egg, beaten, 2 tbsp olive oil
1–2 red chillies (chilies), deseeded and chopped
1 tsp smoked paprika
2 tbsp tomato puree
400 g / 14 oz / 1 ½ cups canned tomatoes
1 tsp sugar
1 tbsp red wine vinegar
4 flatbreads, warmed
spring onions and plain yoghurt, to serve

- Tip the minced chicken into a bowl and use your hands to combine with half the onion and garlic, the coriander and seasoning. Mix in the egg and form into 8 small patties. Refrigerate for 30 minutes.
- Heat the oil in a pan and sauté the remaining onion and garlic with the chillies until golden. Add the paprika and puree and cook out for 2 minutes, stirring, then add the tomatoes and sugar and simmer gently for 20–25 minutes until very thick. Season and stir in the vinegar.
- Heat a little oil in a pan and fry the patties in batches until golden on both sides and cooked through.
- Place the chicken patties on top of warmed flatbreads. Spoon over the tomato sauce and serve with spring onions and some plain yoghurt on top.

Chicken Pittas

504

- Alternatively push the cakes, onions and sauces into warmed split pittas.

505

SERVES 4

Jerk Chicken with Okra

- Blitz the marinade ingredients in a food processor until smooth.
- Coat the chicken thighs and leave to marinate in the refrigerator overnight or for at least 4 hours.
- Pour off any excess marinade and reserve.
- Roast or barbecue the chicken thighs until cooked through and there are no pink juices when pierced with a skewer, about 20–30 minutes.
- Bring the reserved marinade to the boil in a small pan and reduce a little. Add a little salt if necessary.
- Halve the okra lengthways and toss lightly in the seasoned flour and shake off any excess. Heat a thin film of oil in a pan and shallow-fry in batches until crisp-tender.
- Serve the chicken with the fried okra, rice and beans and extra hot sauce for dunking.

Jerk Chicken Wraps

506

- Use tortilla wraps to wrap the shredded meat with lettuce, tomato and a dollop of mayo.

PREPARATION TIME 10 MINUTES
+ MARINATING TIME

COOKING TIME 20–30 MINUTES

....

INGREDIENTS

4 chicken thighs, bone in
200 g / 7 oz / ¾ cup okra
2 tbsp flour, seasoned
vegetable oil

FOR THE MARINADE

4 onions, peeled and sliced
1 scotch bonnet or red chilli (chili), sliced
2 tbsp fresh ginger, grated
1 tsp ground allspice
½ tsp grated nutmeg
½ tsp ground cinnamon
3 garlic cloves, chopped
½ orange, juiced
120 ml / 4 fl. oz / ½ cup white wine vinegar
2 tbsp vegetable oil
rice and beans, to serve

507

SERVES 4

Spicy Indian Chicken Soup

- Heat the olive oil in a large saucepan set over a medium heat. Fry the chicken until golden then remove with a slotted spoon.
- Sweat the onion, carrots, garlic and ginger for 6-8 minutes until soft. Add the ground spices and some salt and pepper. Stir well and cook for a few minutes over a reduced heat.
- Add the tomatoes, stir well then cover with the stock. Simmer for 20–25 minutes until thickened.
- Remove from the heat and remove 3–4 tbsp of the vegetables with a slotted spoon and set aside. Puree the remainder roughly using a stick blender, then return to the heat, add the chicken and reserved vegetables back to the pan and adjust the seasoning to taste.
- Ladle into serving bowls and garnish with coriander before serving.

Indian Lentil Chicken Soup

508

- Add 250 g / 9 oz / 1 ¼ cups lentils for a more substantial soup.

PREPARATION TIME 15 MINUTES

COOKING TIME 35–40 MINUTES

....

INGREDIENTS

50 ml / 1 ½ fl. oz / ¼ cup olive oil
2 chicken breasts, skinned and chopped
1 large onion, finely chopped
2 carrots, peeled and diced
2 cloves garlic, minced
3.5 cm (1 ½ in) piece of ginger, peeled and minced
1 tbsp ground coriander (cilantro)
2 tsp ground cumin
1 tsp Madras curry powder
½ tsp chilli (chili) powder
½ tsp turmeric
400 g / 14 oz / 1 ½ cups canned tomatoes
1 L / 2 pints / 4 cups chicken stock
salt and pepper
coriander (cilantro) leaves, to garnish

509

SERVES 4

Chicken Pappardelle with Tomato

PREPARATION TIME 10 MINUTES

COOKING TIME 10–12 MINUTES

INGREDIENTS

2 tbsp olive oil
4 chicken breasts, skinned and cubed
1 clove of garlic, finely sliced
6 ripe vine tomatoes, cored and chopped
splash of white wine
½ bunch chives, finely chopped
320 g / 11 oz / 1 ¼ cups pappardelle pasta
salt and pepper

- Heat the oil in a pan and cook the chicken until golden and nearly cooked through, about 7 minutes.
- Add the garlic and tomatoes and wine and cook over a low heat until the tomatoes collapse.
- Meanwhile cook the pasta in boiling salted water according to packet instructions. Drain thoroughly, reserving a little pasta water. Toss the pasta and cooking water with the sauce and the chives. Season and serve.

Chicken Pasta with Pesto Sauce

510

- Mix pesto with ricotta and spoon over the top before serving.

511

SERVES 4

Chicken Osso Bucco

PREPARATION TIME 10 MINUTES

COOKING TIME 55 MINUTES

INGREDIENTS

2 tbsp olive oil
4–6 chicken drumsticks
1 onion, chopped
2 cloves of garlic, chopped
1 red pepper, deseeded and sliced
1 green pepper, deseeded and sliced
1 tsp sugar
1 tsp smoked paprika
1 piece orange peel, without white pith
400 g / 14 oz / 1 ½ cups canned tomatoes
250 ml / 9 fl. oz / 1 cup chicken stock
2 bay leaves
1 sprig rosemary
salt and pepper

- Preheat the oven to 180°C (160°C fan) / 350F / gas 4.
- Heat the oil in a pan and brown the drumsticks until golden. Remove to a plate and set aside.
- Add the onion and garlic and cook gently until golden, then add the chicken back to the pan and add the peppers, sugar, paprika, orange peel and seasoning and cook for 5 minutes.
- Pour over the canned tomatoes and stock, add the bay leaves and rosemary, cover with a lid and cook in the oven for 45 minutes until the chicken is cooked.

Gremolata

512

- Finely chop ½ bunch parsley and 1 clove of garlic with some salt and add zest of ½ lemon. Sprinkle over before serving.

513

SERVES 2

Imperial Chicken

Chinese-style Chicken

514

- Try grated ginger; crushed bean sprouts; bamboo shoots; the choice is endless.

Chicken with Szechuan Peppercorns

515

- Szechuan peppercorns add a traditional lip-numbing lick of heat. Sprinkle over to serve.

PREPARATION TIME 10 MINUTES

COOKING TIME 10–15 MINUTES

INGREDIENTS

2 tbsp vegetable oil
2 chicken breasts, skinned and chopped
2 tsp cornflour (cornstarch)
½ onion, peeled and roughly chopped
1 green pepper, deseeded and roughly chopped
½ bunch spring onions (scallions), chopped
2–4 dried chillies (chilies), chopped
1 clove of garlic, finely sliced
2 tbsp Chinese rice wine
4 tbsp soy sauce
100 ml / 3 ½ fl. oz / ½ cup chicken stock
handful of unsalted cashew nuts

- Heat the oil in a wok until smoking. Toss the chicken in cornflour, shake off the excess and fry quickly until golden.
- Add the onion, pepper, spring onions and chillies, then the garlic and stir fry for 2 minutes.
- Add the rice wine, reduce, then add the soy and stock and cashews and simmer for 5 minutes.
- Serve in deep bowls.

516

SERVES 4

Chicken Curry with Rice

PREPARATION TIME 15 MINUTES

COOKING TIME 45 MINUTES

INGREDIENTS

3 tbsp vegetable oil
1 onion, peeled and finely sliced
1 red pepper, deseeded and finely chopped
2 cloves of garlic, chopped
1 tsp fresh ginger, grated
1 tsp ground coriander (cilantro)
½ tsp turmeric
1 tsp ground cumin
1 tbsp garam masala
1 tsp paprika
4 chicken breasts, skinned and thickly sliced
100 g / 3 ½ oz / ½ cup plain yoghurt
salt
coriander (cilantro) leaves, to garnish
250 g / 9 oz / 1 cup rice
100 g / 3 ½ oz / ½ cup frozen peas

- Heat the oil in a pan and sauté the onion and pepper for about 10 minutes or until golden-brown. Add the garlic and ginger and fry for another minute.
- Add the spices and stir well, then add 200 ml / 7 fl. oz / ¾ cup water and cook gently for 10 minutes or so.
- Add the chicken to the sauce and top up with 300 ml / ½ pint / 1 ¼ cups water. Cook at a simmer for around 20 minutes until the chicken is tender.
- Meanwhile cook the rice according to packet instructions, adding the peas for the last 5 minutes of cooking. Drain thoroughly.
- Stir the yoghurt into the curry and heat through without boiling.
- Season and sprinkle with coriander leaves before serving on top of the rice.

517

SERVES 2

Chicken Artichoke Tagine

PREPARATION TIME 10 MINUTES

COOKING TIME 55 MINUTES

INGREDIENTS

2 globe artichokes
1 lemon, juiced
2 tbsp olive oil
1 onion, peeled and finely sliced
2 cloves of garlic, finely sliced
4 chicken thighs, skinned
1 tsp ras-el-hanout spice mix
1 tsp ground coriander (cilantro) seeds
4 preserved lemons, chopped
300 ml / 10 fl. oz / 1 ¼ cups chicken stock
4 ripe tomatoes, quartered
salt and pepper
chopped parsley, to serve

- Prepare the artichokes: Remove around 4–5 of the toughest outer leaves. Place the artichoke at the edge of the table so the stalk hangs over the edge. Snap away the stem, removing some of the tough fibres running into the base.
- Remove the inedible choke: Spread the leaves apart until you come to the central thinner, lighter leaves. Pull this cone out in one piece and underneath will be the hairy choke, scrape out with a teaspoon.
- Rinse the artichokes with water and place immediately in a bowl of water with lemon juice to prevent discolouring.
- Heat the oil in a large pan and cook the onions until golden and tender.
- Add the garlic and cook for a few minutes, then remove all from the pan with a slotted spoon.
- Increase the heat and brown the chicken on all sides, then tip the onions back into the pan and sprinkle over the spices. Add the artichoke halves into the pan with the tomatoes and lemons.
- Pour over the stock and season, lower the heat and cook gently for about 45 minutes or until the sauce has thickened and the chicken is cooked. Serve scattered with parsley.

518
SERVES 6

Chicken Yassa with Rice

- Marinate the chicken in the lemon juice, onions, seasoning, chilli and a little oil for at least 4 hours.
- Preheat the oven to 200°C (180°C fan) / 400F / gas 6.
- Shake off any excess marinade and roast the chicken pieces in the oven for 20 minutes or so until golden.
- Meanwhile cook 2 onions from the marinade in 1 tbsp oil in a pan until tender, then add the remaining marinade and heat through. Add the browned chicken, habanero, olives, mustard and 100 ml / 3 ½ fl. oz / ¾ cup water and simmer for 20 minutes until the chicken is cooked through.
- Heat the olive oil in a separate pan and caramelise the remaining onion with turmeric and sugar.
- Remove the habanero from the curry. Serve the rice with the caramelised onion on top and the chicken alongside.

PREPARATION TIME 5 MINUTES
+ MARINATING TIME
COOKING TIME 40 MINUTES

INGREDIENTS

2 tbsp lemon juice, salt and pepper
3 onions, peeled and finely sliced
1 red chilli (chili), finely chopped
1 chicken, jointed into 6 pieces
2 tbsp peanut or groundnut oil
1 habanero chilli (chili),
½ oz / ½ cup green olives
1 tbsp Dijon mustard
2 tbsp olive oil
½ tsp turmeric, ½ tsp sugar
cooked white rice

519
SERVES 4

Chicken and Almond Curry

PREPARATION TIME 15 MINUTES
COOKING TIME 30 MINUTES

INGREDIENTS

2 tbsp olive oil
4 chicken breasts, chopped
1 onion
1 stick celery, 2 cloves of garlic
1 cm (½ in) piece fresh ginger

4 tomatoes, cored and diced
1 tbsp flour
1 tsp paprika
1 tsp Cayenne pepper
400 g / 14 oz / 1 ½ cups coconut milk
100 ml / 3 ½ fl. oz / ½ cup chicken stock
100 g / 3 ½ oz / ½ cup flaked (slivered) almonds
1 bay leaf, salt and pepper

- Peel and chop the onion. Finely chop the celery, garlic and ginger.
- Heat the oil in a large pan and cook the chicken until golden then remove and set aside. Sauté the onion and celery until softened.
- Add the garlic, ginger and flour and cook out for a few seconds, then add the chicken back to the pan.
- Sprinkle over the spices, then pour in coconut milk and stock. Add the bay leaf and season, then simmer for about 20 minutes over a low heat until the sauce has thickened and the chicken is cooked.
- Serve decorated with the almonds.

520
SERVES 4

Teriyaki Chicken with Asparagus

PREPARATION TIME 25 MINUTES
+ MARINATING TIME
COOKING TIME 20 MINUTES

INGREDIENTS

2 chicken breasts, skinned and sliced
4 tbsp teriyaki sauce

1 tbsp soy sauce
1 tsp sugar
300 g / 10 oz / 1 ¼ cups Japanese rice, washed
500 ml / 1 pint / 2 cups water
1 tbsp vegetable oil
1 tsp sesame oil
1 tbsp sesame seeds
1 bunch asparagus, trimmed

- Toss the chicken in the sauces and sugar and leave for 20 minutes.
- Meanwhile place the rice and water in a pan, cover and simmer for 15 minutes. Turn the heat to low and simmer for about 5 minutes with the lid off to evaporate all the water. Taste and check the rice is cooked.
- Heat the oils in a wok and stir-fry the chicken until cooked through, about 5–6 minutes, then toss in the sesame seeds.
- Steam the asparagus over simmering water for 4 minutes until just tender.
- Serve the chicken on top of the rice, the asparagus alongside.

521

SERVES 2

Chicken with Broccoli

PREPARATION TIME 10 MINUTES

COOKING TIME 15 MINUTES

INGREDIENTS

1 tbsp vegetable oil
2 chicken breasts, skinned and
roughly chopped
1 head of broccoli, separated
into florets
1 bunch of spring onions
(scallions), sliced
2 cloves of garlic, finely sliced
2 tbsp soy sauce
½ tsp cornflour (cornstarch)
dissolved in 1 tbsp water
1 star anise
black pepper
cooked rice, to serve

- Heat the oil in a wok and stir fry the chicken briskly until golden. Add the vegetables, garlic, soy, dissolved cornflour and star anise and reduce the heat.
- Bubble up until the sauce is slightly thickened and glossy and the chicken is cooked. The broccoli should retain some bite.
- Serve the chicken with the vegetables on top of cooked rice.

Chicken with Mange Tout 522

- Replace the broccoli with mange tout.

523

SERVES 2

Chicken and Spring Vegetables

PREPARATION TIME 10 MINUTES

COOKING TIME 25–30 MINUTES

INGREDIENTS

2 chicken breasts, skin on
400 g / 14 oz / 1 ½ cups waxy
potatoes, quartered
1 bunch baby carrots, scrubbed
and trimmed
3 tbsp olive oil
40 g / 1 oz butter
2 sprigs thyme
salt and pepper
150 g / 5 oz / ⅔ cup sugar snap peas
500 g / 1 lb / 2 cups spinach leaves

- Preheat the oven to 200°C (180°C fan) / 400F / gas 6.
- Arrange the chicken, potatoes and carrots in a roasting tin, dot with butter and oil, sprinkle over thyme leaves, season and roast for 25 minutes until golden and caramelised.
- Meanwhile steam the sugar snap peas over simmering water for 4–5 minutes until tender.
- Wilt the spinach in a pan with 1 tbsp water.
- Thickly slice the chicken and toss all the vegetables gently together with the roasting juices from the pan.

Chicken with Spring Vegetables and Rice 524

- Serve on a bed of boiled rice.

525

SERVES 4

Summer Chicken and Vegetable Crumble

- Heat 40 g butter in a pan and sauté the chicken, onion, courgette and peppers until golden. Add the tomatoes and mange tout and simmer for 20 minutes until thickened then season and set aside.
- Meanwhile rub the cold butter and semolina or couscous together with your fingertips to resemble large breadcrumbs, then stir through the pine nuts and season well.
- Spoon the chicken mixture into a gratin dish, then top lightly with the crumble. Grill or bake until bubbling and the topping is golden and crunchy.

Creamy Chicken Crumble

526

- Stir in 2 tbsp cream cheese or crème fraiche for an indulgent version on a cool night.

PREPARATION TIME 15 MINUTES

COOKING TIME 30–40 MINUTES

INGREDIENTS

40g / 1 oz butter
4 chicken breasts, skinned and cubed
1 onion, peeled and chopped
1 yellow pepper, deseeded and roughly chopped
1 red pepper, deseeded and roughly chopped
1 courgette (zucchini), sliced
100 g / 3 ½ oz / ½ cup mange tout
400 g / 14 oz / 1 ½ cups canned tomatoes
salt and pepper
120 g / 4 oz / ½ cup semolina or couscous
100 g / 3 ½ oz / ½ cup butter, cold and cubed
50 g / 1 ¾ oz / ¼ cup pine nuts, chopped

527

SERVES 4

Chicken Tagine with Oranges and Olives

- Heat the oil in a large pan and cook the onions until golden and tender.
- Add the garlic and cook for a few minutes, then remove all from the pan with a slotted spoon.
- Increase the heat and brown the chicken on all sides, add the courgette, then tip the onions back into the pan and sprinkle over the spices. Add the orange peel.
- Pour over the stock and season, lower the heat and cook gently for about 45 minutes or until the sauce has thickened and the chicken is cooked.
- Add the orange wedges to warm through, adjust the seasoning and serve sprinkled with coriander.

Chicken with Lemon and Olives

528

- Replace the orange with lemon.

PREPARATION TIME 15 MINUTES

COOKING TIME 55 MINUTES

INGREDIENTS

2 tbsp olive oil
1 onion, peeled and finely sliced
2 cloves of garlic, finely sliced
4 chicken legs, skinned
1 courgette (zucchini), chopped
1 tsp ras-el-hanout spice mix
1 tsp ground coriander (cilantro) seeds
1 orange, cut into thin wedges + 1 piece orange peel
400 ml / 14 fl. oz / 1 ½ cups chicken stock
2 tbsp olives
salt and pepper
chopped coriander (cilantro), to garnish

529

SERVES 2

Vietnamese Chicken Fricassee

PREPARATION TIME 10 MINUTES

COOKING TIME 10–15 MINUTES

INGREDIENTS

1 tbsp vegetable oil
1 onion, peeled and finely sliced
2 cloves of garlic, finely sliced
2 chicken breasts, skinned and cubed
1–2 green chillies (chilies), chopped
100 ml / 3 ½ fl. oz / ¾ cup chicken stock
2 tbsp soy sauce
1–2 tsp sugar
½ bunch Thai basil
steamed rice, to serve

- Heat the oil in a wok and stir fry the onion until deep gold. Add the garlic, chillies and chicken and stir fry until the chicken is cooked through. Add the stock and cook until bubbling.
- Add the soy and sugar and reduce until caramelised and sticky and coating the chicken.
- Stir through the basil and serve with the rice.

Vietnamese Prawn and Chicken Fricassee

 530

- Add raw king prawns to the wok as well as the chicken.

531

SERVES 4

Chicken with Padron Peppers

PREPARATION TIME 10 MINUTES

COOKING TIME 35–40 MINUTES

INGREDIENTS

2 tbsp olive oil
4 chicken drumsticks
1 onion, peeled and sliced
2 cloves of garlic, finely sliced
200 g / 7 oz / ¾ cup padron peppers or green peppers, chopped
8 ripe tomatoes, cored and diced
salt and pepper

- Heat the oil in a casserole and brown the chicken on all sides.
- Add the onion and garlic, fry until golden, then add the padron peppers. Cook until everything is slightly caught and golden, then add the tomatoes, a glass of water and seasoning, cover with a lid and simmer for 20 minutes or until the chicken is cooked.
- Adjust the seasoning and serve

Chicken with Peppers and Couscous

 532

- Serve on a bed of couscous.

533

SERVES 4

Chicken with Peppers and Sesame Seeds

Chicken with Steamed Rice

534

- Steamed rice would stretch this meal even further for unexpected company.

Stuffed Aubergines

535

- Hollow out halved aubergines, bake in the oven until tender then stuff with the mixture.

PREPARATION TIME 10 MINUTES

COOKING TIME 10–12 MINUTES

INGREDIENTS

2 tbsp vegetable oil
1 tsp sesame oil
350 g / 12 oz / 1 ½ cups chicken thigh meat, diced
1 onion, peeled and chopped
2 cloves of garlic, finely sliced
1 tsp fresh ginger, grated
1 red pepper, deseeded and finely sliced
1 green pepper, deseeded and finely sliced
200 g / 7 oz / ¾ cup bamboo shoots
handful fresh or frozen peas
2–3 tbsp sweet and sour sauce
2–3 tbsp black sesame seeds
salt and pepper

- Heat the oils in a wok until nearly smoking, then add the chicken. Stir-fry over a high heat until golden all over. Remove from the pan with a slotted spoon.

- Add the onion, garlic and ginger and stir-fry for 2 minutes. Add the vegetables and cook until crisp-tender. Add the meat back to the pan and stir in the sauce.

- Leave to bubble for a few minutes then, toss in the sesame seeds, check and adjust the seasoning if necessary.

536

SERVES 4

Sweet and Sour Chicken

PREPARATION TIME 15 MINUTES

COOKING TIME 20 MINUTES

....

INGREDIENTS

500 g / 1 lb / 2 cups chicken thigh
meat, sliced
1 tbsp vegetable oil
1 carrot, peeled and cut into
matchsticks
1 red pepper, deseeded and finely
sliced
1 red onion, peeled and thickly sliced
50 g / 1 ¾ oz / ¼ cup pineapple
chunks

FOR THE SAUCE

125 ml / 4 fl. oz / ½ cup pineapple
juice
splash dry sherry or Shaoxing
rice wine
2 tbsp ketchup
2 tbsp soy sauce
2 tbsp Chinese vinegar or red
wine vinegar
1 tsp cornflour (cornstarch)

- Heat the vegetable oil in a wok until smoking, then add the chicken and stir fry over a high heat until the chicken turns white.
- Remove the chicken from the pan and set aside.
- Heat the oil in the wok again and stir fry the vegetables over a high heat for 4 minutes.
- Mix together the sauce ingredients with the cornflour. Add the chicken back to the pan with the pineapple and sauce, bubble up until thickened and serve with white rice.

Sweet and Sour Chicken and Prawns

537

- Add king prawns as well as the chicken.

538

SERVES 4

Spicy Chicken with Herbs

PREPARATION TIME 10 MINUTES

COOKING TIME 20–25 MINUTES

....

INGREDIENTS

4 chicken breasts, roughly chopped
2 tbsp vegetable oil
1 shallot, finely chopped
1 clove of garlic, finely chopped
1–2 green chillies (chilies), sliced
1 bay leaf
1 cinnamon stick
½ bunch coriander (cilantro),
chopped
400 ml / 14 fl. oz / 1 ½ cups coconut
milk
½ lime, juiced
salt and pepper

- Heat the oil in a wok and stir fry the chicken until golden.
- Add the shallot, garlic and chillies and fry for 2 minutes, then add the bay leaf, cinnamon stick, coriander and coconut milk and simmer for 10–15 minutes until the chicken is cooked through.
- Squeeze over the lime, adjust the seasoning and serve, removing the cinnamon stick if you can find it.

Spicy Chicken with Chilli Sauce

539

- Drizzle with sweet chilli (chili) sauce before serving for an extra kick.

540

SERVES 4

Chicken Jambalaya

- Heat the oil in a pan and fry the onion, garlic and celery until golden.
- Add the chorizo and fry until the fat starts to run, then add the chicken, chilli and rice and stir to coat thoroughly.
- Pour over the stock, bring to a simmer, turn down the heat and leave to cook for about 15 minutes.
- Stir in the tomatoes and peas and cook until the peas are tender, about 5–6 minutes.
- Season with hot sauce, lemon juice and salt and pepper before serving scattered with thyme leaves.

PREPARATION TIME 10 MINUTES

COOKING TIME 30 MINUTES

INGREDIENTS

2 tbsp olive oil
1 onion, peeled and finely sliced
2 cloves of garlic, finely chopped
2 stalks of celery, finely chopped
100 g / 4 oz / ⅓ cup chorizo sausage, diced
2 chicken breasts, skinned and diced
1 chilli (chili), deseeded and finely chopped
200 g / 7 oz / ¾ cup white basmati rice
600 ml / 1 ¼ pints / 2 ½ cups chicken stock
2 ripe tomatoes, chopped
50 g / 1 ¾ oz / ¼ cup frozen peas
hot sauce
1 lemon, juiced
salt and pepper
thyme leaves, to garnish

Jambalaya Chicken and Prawns

541

- Add cooked king prawns as well as the chicken.

542

SERVES 4

Creamy Chicken with Rice

- Heat the oil in a pan and fry the chicken until white on both sides. Remove with a slotted spoon.
- Add the shallot and sweat without colouring, then return the chicken to the pan with the curry powder, mango chutney and cream. Simmer for 5–10 minutes until the chicken is cooked. Season.
- Tip the rice into a pan with the water and cook covered with a lid for 10 minutes. Remove from the heat and leave covered for 5 minutes.
- Serve the chicken with the sauce spooned over and peppercorns sprinkled on top.

PREPARATION TIME 5 MINUTES

COOKING TIME 15–20 MINUTES

INGREDIENTS

2 tbsp vegetable oil
4 chicken breasts, skinned
1 shallot, finely diced
1 tbsp curry powder
1 tbsp mango chutney
200 ml / 7 fl. oz / ¾ cup double (heavy) cream
salt and pepper
250 g / 9 oz / 1 cup basmati rice
500 ml / 1 pint / 2 cups water
1 tbsp Szechuan peppercorns

Old-school Chicken Curry

543

- Add sultanas, a handful of shaved coconut and almonds for a flashback to the 70s.

544

SERVES 4

Chicken Korma

Chicken Korma with Mango

545

- Add ½ a finely diced ripe mango 10 minutes before the end of cooking for a fruity finish.

Chicken Korma with Paneer

546

- For a more savoury finish, add 125 g / 4 ½ oz / 1 cup paneer cheese 10 minutes before the end of cooking.

PREPARATION TIME 30 MINUTES

COOKING TIME 50 MINUTES

INGREDIENTS

450 g / 1 lb skinless chicken breast, cubed
2 tbsp korma curry powder
2 tbsp olive oil
1 onion, finely chopped
1 red chilli (chili), finely chopped
2 cloves of garlic, crushed
200 g / 7 oz / 1 cup canned tomatoes, chopped
400 ml/ 14 fl. oz / 1 ⅔ cups coconut milk
4 tbsp ground almonds
2 tbsp mango chutney

- Mix the chicken breast pieces with the curry powder and leave to marinate for 30 minutes.
- Heat the oil in a large saucepan and fry the onion and chilli for 3 minutes, stirring occasionally.
- Add the garlic and cook for 2 minutes or until the mustard seeds start to pop.
- Add the chicken and cook for 4 minutes, stirring occasionally, until it starts to colour on the outside.
- Add the chopped tomatoes, coconut milk, ground almonds and mango chutney and bring to a gentle simmer.
- Cook the curry for 35 minutes, stirring occasionally, until the chicken is tender and the sauce has thickened.

547

SERVES 4

Spicy Sticky Chicken

- Mix together all the ingredients except the chicken and lime wedges, tasting as you go. You may want it spicier or sweeter.
- Coat the chicken thoroughly and marinate for 30 minutes.
- Preheat the oven to 190°C (170°C fan) / 375F / gas 5.
- Cook the chicken in a foil-lined roasting tin for about 30 minutes or until dark golden and sticky.
- Serve with lime wedges.

PREPARATION TIME 10 MINUTES
+ MARINATING TIME

COOKING TIME 30 MINUTES

INGREDIENTS

4 chicken thighs
2 tbsp runny honey
2 tbsp tomato ketchup
1–2 tbsp Worcestershire sauce
1 tbsp Dijon mustard
hot sauce
salt and pepper
1 tbsp vegetable oil
lime wedges to serve

Szechuan Sticky Chicken

548

- Add 1 tbsp crushed Szechuan peppercorns to the chicken for their lip-tingling heat.

549

SERVES 4

Spicy Chicken Kebabs with Glazed Vegetables

- Marinate the chicken in a bowl with chilli, oregano, lemon juice and half the oil for 30 minutes.
- Heat the remaining oil in a pan and sauté the vegetables until just tender, then toss in the balsamic vinegar. Season and keep warm.
- Thread the chicken onto soaked wooden skewers, then griddle over high heat for 6–8 minutes until cooked through and golden.
- Serve the kebabs with the balsamic glazed vegetables.

PREPARATION TIME 10 MINUTES

COOKING TIME 15 MINUTES

INGREDIENTS

4 chicken thighs, skinned, deboned and chopped
1 red chilli (chili), finely chopped
2 tsp dried oregano
½ lemon, juiced
4 tbsp olive oil
salt
1 courgette (zucchini), cut into thin batons
1 red pepper, deseeded and sliced
1 yellow pepper, deseeded and sliced
1 tbsp balsamic vinegar

Balsamic Chicken Kebabs

550

- Swap the flavourings over: Marinate the chicken in balsamic and sauté the vegetables with chilli, oregano and lemon.

551

SERVES 4

Grilled Spicy Chicken in Lemon Leaves

PREPARATION TIME 10 MINUTES

COOKING TIME 20–30 MINUTES

INGREDIENTS

4 chicken thighs, skinned and deboned
1 red chilli (chili), finely sliced
1 tbsp fresh ginger, finely sliced
2 cloves of garlic, finely sliced
2 tbsp huoc nam or fish sauce
1–2 tsp sugar
1 lime, juiced
lemon or banana leaves

- Mix together the chilli, ginger, garlic, huoc nam and sugar with some lime juice and taste - you need a balance of hot, sharp and sweet.
- Toss the chicken in the marinade and refrigerate for 1 hour.
- Wrap the chicken in the leaves. Heat a griddle pan until hot.
- Griddle the parcels over the heat until charred and the chicken is cooked through.
- You could bubble up any remaining marinade in a small pan to serve as a dipping sauce.

Griddled Chicken with Lime 552

- Add sliced lime tucked under the chicken for extra freshness.

553

SERVES 4

Basque Chicken

PREPARATION TIME 10 MINUTES

COOKING TIME 30 MINUTES

INGREDIENTS

2 tbsp olive oil
4 chicken drumsticks
1 onion, chopped
2 cloves of garlic, chopped
1 red pepper, deseeded and sliced
1 green pepper, deseeded and sliced
6 ripe vine tomatoes, cored and chopped
2 bay leaves
1 tsp sugar
1 tsp smoked paprika
salt and pepper
rice or mashed potato, to serve

- Heat the oil in a pan and brown the drumsticks until golden. Remove to a plate and set aside.
- Add the onion and garlic and cook gently until golden, then add the chicken back to the pan and add the peppers and tomatoes, bay leaves, sugar, paprika and seasoning and allow to simmer for about 10–15 minutes until all is combined. Adjust the seasoning.
- Serve hot with your choice of accompaniment.

Oven Baked Basque Chicken 554

- Add 100 ml / 3 ½ oz / ¾ cup water or stock, some chopped carrots and transfer to a lidded casserole dish and cook slowly for an hour.

SERVES 4

Chicken with Spices and Chocolate

555

- Heat the oil in a pan and fry the chicken skin side down until crisp and golden.
- Turn over, add the onion and spices and cook until the onion is golden and the chicken just cooked through. Remove from the pan with a slotted spoon.
- Pour in the cream, bubble up and add the chocolate cut into chunks. Stir until thickened and smooth, season carefully and serve alongside the chicken.

PREPARATION TIME 10 MINUTES

COOKING TIME 20 MINUTES

INGREDIENTS

4 chicken breasts, skin on
2 tbsp vegetable oil
1 onion, peeled and finely sliced
1 stick cinnamon
1 red chilli (chili), finely sliced
150 ml / 5 fl. oz / ⅔ cup single cream
75–100 g / 2 ½ - 3 ½ oz / ⅓ - ½ cup dark chocolate
salt and pepper

Cheese with Chocolate Sauce

556

- Try serving the chocolate sauce with some grilled halloumi cheese.

SERVES 4

Chicken Stir-fry Salad

557

- Heat the oil in a wok until nearly smoking, then add the chicken. Stir fry over a high heat until golden all over and the fat crisp. Remove from the pan with a slotted spoon.
- Meanwhile steam the broccoli florets and carrots for 2 minutes, then remove from the heat.
- Add the onion, garlic and ginger to the wok and stir fry for 2 minutes. Add the remaining vegetables including the broccoli and carrots and cook until crisp-tender.
- Add the meat back to the pan and stir in the sauces. Leave to bubble for a few minutes then check and adjust the seasoning if necessary.
- Serve warm or at room temperature.

PREPARATION TIME 10 MINUTES

COOKING TIME 10–12 MINUTES

INGREDIENTS

2 tbsp vegetable oil
350 g / 12 oz / 1 ½ cups chicken thigh meat, diced
1 head broccoli, separated into florets
2 carrots, peeled and sliced
1 onion, peeled and finely sliced
2 cloves of garlic, finely sliced
1 tsp fresh ginger, grated
1 yellow pepper, deseeded and chopped
150 g / 5 oz / ⅔ cup mushrooms, sliced
200 g / 7 oz / ¾ cup beansprouts
75–100 ml / 2 ½–3 ½ fl. oz / ⅓–½ cup soy sauce
2–3 tbsp oyster sauce
salt and pepper

Chicken and Squid Stir-fry

558

- Rings of squid, added with the chicken, would add texture and interest to the dish.

559

SERVES 2

Bulgarian Chicken Salad

PREPARATION TIME 10 MINUTES

COOKING TIME 20 MINUTES

INGREDIENTS

2 chicken breasts
½ red onion, peeled and finely diced
1 yellow pepper, deseeded and
finely diced
400 g / 14 oz / 1 ½ cups baby
spinach leaves
1 lemon
salt and pepper

- Poach the chicken breasts in simmering water very gently for about 20 minutes until just cooked through. Set aside to cool.
- Mix the diced onion and peppers with spinach. Use a zester to take the yellow rind off a lemon, no white pith, and add to the vegetables. Toss with a little of the juice.
- Slice the chicken and serve with the salad.

560

SERVES 4

Chicken Kebabs with Lassi

PREPARATION TIME 20 MINUTES
+ MARINATING TIME

COOKING TIME 20 MINUTES

INGREDIENTS

4 chicken thighs, skinned, deboned
and cut into chunks
½ onion, peeled and chopped
2-3 green chillies (chilies), deseeded,
chopped
3 cloves of garlic, peeled
2 tsp fresh ginger, chopped
1 tsp ground cumin
1 tsp ground coriander (cilantro)
1 tbsp dried mint
80 g / 2 ½ oz / ⅓ cup plain yoghurt
saffron rice, to serve

FOR THE LASSI
200 ml / 7 fl. oz / ¾ cup single cream
400 ml / 14 fl. oz / 1 ½ cups milk
800 ml / 1 ¾ pints / 3 ⅓ cups plain
yoghurt
400 g / 14 oz / 1 ½ cups fruit pulp,
such as mango
caster (superfine) sugar

- Pat the chicken dry with kitchen paper.
- Whiz the onion, chillies, garlic, ginger, herbs, spices and yoghurt in a food processor until smooth. Toss the chicken in the paste and leave to marinate in the refrigerator for at least 1 hour or overnight.
- When ready to serve, whizz the ingredients for the lassi in a blender until smooth. Taste to see how much sugar you need. Chill in the refrigerator.
- Shake off any excess marinade from the chicken and thread onto skewers and cook either on a barbecue or very hot griddle pan until charred on the outside and cooked in the centre, about 5–6 minutes.
- Serve with saffron rice and the lassi.

561
SERVES 4

Basque Chicken and Pepper Casserole

- Preheat the oven to 180°C (160°C fan) / 350F / gas 4.
- Chop the onion and garlic.
- Heat the oil in a pan and brown the thighs until golden. Remove to a plate and set aside.
- Add the onion and garlic and cook gently until golden, then add the chicken back to the pan and add the peppers, sugar, paprika, Espelette pepper and seasoning and cook for 5 minutes.
- Pour over the canned tomatoes and stock, add the bay leaves and some salt, cover with a lid and cook in the oven for 45 minutes until the chicken is cooked.

PREPARATION TIME 10 MINUTES

COOKING TIME 55 MINUTES

....

INGREDIENTS

2 tbsp olive oil
4–6 chicken thighs
1 onion, 2 cloves of garlic
1 red pepper, deseeded and sliced
1 green pepper, deseeded and sliced
1 tsp sugar
1 tsp smoked paprika
1 tsp Espelette pepper
400 g / 14 oz / 1 ½ cups canned tomatoes
250 ml / 9 fl. oz / 1 cup chicken stock
2 bay leaves, salt

Coconut Milk Chicken Soup

562
SERVES 4

Chicken and Pear Curry

563
SERVES 4

PREPARATION TIME 15 MINUTES

COOKING TIME 25–30 MINUTES

....

INGREDIENTS

3 tbsp vegetable oil
1 onion, peeled and finely sliced
2 cloves of garlic, finely chopped
1 red chilli (chili), finely sliced
3–4 chicken breasts, skinned and cubed

2 tsp tamarind paste
2 tbsp fish sauce
400 ml / 14 fl. oz / 1 ½ cups coconut milk
200 ml / 7 fl. oz / ¾ cup chicken stock
salt and pepper
1–2 limes, juiced
½ bunch coriander (cilantro), finely chopped, stalks reserved

- Heat the oil in a wok or large pan and fry the onion until deep gold and sweet.
- Add the garlic and chilli and cook out for 2 minutes.
- Add the cubed chicken and allow to colour on all sides.
- Stir in the tamarind and fish sauce, then pour over the coconut milk and chicken stock and add the coriander stalks.
- Lower the heat and leave to simmer for 15–20 minutes until the chicken is cooked through.
- Adjust the seasoning and stir in the lime juice and chopped coriander just before serving.

PREPARATION TIME 10 MINUTES

COOKING TIME 30 MINUTES

....

INGREDIENTS

2 tbsp vegetable oil
4 chicken thighs, skin on
1 onion, peeled and finely sliced
4 pears, quartered and cored

2 yellow peppers, deseeded and finely sliced
½ tsp turmeric
1 tsp ground cinnamon
1 tsp ground cumin
350 ml / 12 fl. oz / 1 ½ cups chicken stock
salt and pepper

- Heat the oil in a pan and brown the chicken thighs on all sides, then remove to a plate.
- Add the onion and cook until golden and soft, then add the pears and peppers and cook for 5 minutes until softening.
- Add the chicken back to the pan with the spices and stir to coat, then pour in the stock. Simmer for 20 minutes or until the chicken is cooked through.
- Adjust the seasoning and serve.

564

SERVES 4 # Moroccan Chicken with Couscous

PREPARATION TIME 15 MINUTES

COOKING TIME 30 MINUTES

INGREDIENTS

2 tbsp olive oil
4 chicken breasts, skinned
1 yellow pepper, diced
1 red pepper, diced
1 courgette (zucchini), diced
1 ½ tsp ras el hanout spice mix
100 g / 3 ½ oz / ½ cup black olives
400 g / 14 oz / 1 ½ cups canned
tomatoes
salt and pepper
250 g / 9 oz / 1 cup couscous
250 ml / 9 fl. oz / 1 cup chicken
or vegetable stock
60 g / 2 oz / ¼ cup raisins
squeeze of lemon juice

- Heat the oil in a pan and fry the chicken until golden, then remove with a slotted spoon and set aside.
- Add the vegetables and sauté until starting to soften, then add the spice mix and cook for 1 minute. Add the chicken back to the pan, toss to coat, then add the olives and tomatoes and simmer for 20 minutes or until all is tender and the chicken is cooked. Season.
- Place the couscous in a bowl, add the raisins, cover with the hot stock and cling film the bowl. Leave for 10 minutes or so until tender, then fork through the grains and add the lemon.
- Remove the chicken and cut into slices. Serve the hot stew and chicken alongside the couscous.

Chicken with Baked Potato
 565

- Serve the chicken on top of a baked potato.

566

SERVES 4 # Wok-fried Chicken and Vegetables

PREPARATION TIME 10 MINUTES

COOKING TIME 10–12 MINUTES

INGREDIENTS

2 tbsp vegetable oil
350 g / 12 oz / 1 ½ cups chicken
thigh meat, diced
1 head broccoli, separated into
florets
2 carrots, peeled and sliced
2 cloves of garlic, finely sliced
1 tsp fresh ginger, grated
½ bunch spring onions (scallions),
finely sliced
150 g / 5 oz / ⅔ cup mushrooms,
sliced
200 g / 7 oz / ¾ cup beansprouts
75–100 ml / 2 ½–3 ½ fl. oz / ⅓–½ cup
soy sauce
2–3 tbsp oyster sauce or hoisin sauce
salt and pepper

- Heat the oil in a wok until nearly smoking, then add the chicken. Stir-fry over a high heat until golden all over and the fat crisp. Remove from the pan with a slotted spoon.
- Meanwhile steam the broccoli florets and carrots for 2 minutes, then remove from the heat.
- Add the spring onions, garlic and ginger to the wok and stir-fry for 2 minutes. Add the remaining vegetables including the broccoli and carrots and cook until crisp-tender.
- Add the meat back to the pan and stir in the sauces. Leave to bubble for a few minutes then check and adjust the seasoning if necessary.
- Serve immediately.

Wok-fried Chicken and Noodles
567

- Serve on a bed of cooked noodles.

568

SERVES 4

Chicken and Galangal Soup

- Heat the oil in a pan and sweat the onion and garlic without colouring.
- Add galangal, lemongrass, curry and lime leaves and chilli and cook for a few minutes until the scent is released, then pour in the coconut milk and stock.
- When simmering, add the chicken pieces and simmer gently for 15 minutes or until the chicken is cooked.
- Season the soup with the fish sauce and lime juice and serve sprinkled with coriander, red onion, chilli and spring onion.

PREPARATION TIME 10 MINUTES

COOKING TIME 25 MINUTES

INGREDIENTS

1 tbsp vegetable oil
1 onion, peeled and finely sliced
2 cloves of garlic, finely sliced
2 cm piece galangal, finely sliced
1 stalk lemongrass, bruised
3 curry leaves
2 lime leaves
1 red chilli (chili), finely sliced
400 ml / 14 fl. oz / 1 ½ cups coconut milk
250 ml / 9 fl. oz / 1 cup chicken stock
2 chicken breasts, skinned and sliced
2 tbsp fish sauce
1 lime, juiced
½ bunch fresh coriander (cilantro), chopped
sliced red onion, red chilli and spring onions to garnish

Chicken Galangal Curry

569

- Reduce the liquid by half and serve over white rice as a curry.

570

SERVES 4

Chicken Tikka in Chicory Boats

- Cube the chicken, toss with the curry paste and yoghurt and leave to marinate in the refrigerator for 30 minutes.
- Wipe off any excess marinade. Griddle or fry the chicken in a pan until golden and sizzling and just cooked through.
- Scrape any excess marinade into a pan, loosen with a tbsp water and heat very gently without boiling.
- Fill the chicory leaves with chopped herbs and sesame seeds then sit the cooked chicken on top. Squeeze over a little lemon juice and seasoning and serve with the marinade dip.

PREPARATION TIME 5 MINUTES
+ MARINATING TIME

COOKING TIME 10 MINUTES

INGREDIENTS

4 chicken breasts, skinned
4 tbsp tikka masala paste
200 ml / 7 fl.oz / ¾ cup plain yoghurt
salt and pepper
2 heads chicory, leaves separated
½ bunch parsley or coriander (cilantro), chopped
2 tbsp sesame seeds
½ lemon, juiced

Chicken Tikka with a Mint Yoghurt

571

- For cool contrast, mix a few tbsp plain yoghurt with chopped mint, a crushed clove of garlic and some grated cucumber.

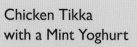

572
SERVES 4

Chicken with Couscous

PREPARATION TIME 10 MINUTES
COOKING TIME
1 HOUR 20 MINUTES

....

INGREDIENTS

olive oil
2 onions, peeled and sliced
4 cloves of garlic, finely sliced
4 merguez sausages
2 carrots, peeled and sliced
400 g / 14 oz / 1 ½ cups chickpeas
400 g / 14 oz / 1 ½ cups tomatoes
500 ml / 1 pint / 2 cups chicken stock
50 g / 1 ¾ oz / ¼ cup dates
2 tbsp honey
225 g / 8 oz / 1 cup couscous
225 ml / 8 fl. oz / 1 cup chicken stock

FOR THE SPICE RUB
4 chicken legs
½ tsp cayenne, 1 tbsp paprika
1 tsp turmeric, salt and pepper
2 tsp ground cinnamon
1 tbsp ground cumin

- Preheat the oven to 160°C (140°C fan) / 325F / gas 3.
- Mix the spices for the rub in a bowl and toss the chicken legs in half of the spice mix. Marinate overnight.
- The next day heat 2 tbsp oil in a large casserole or tagine and cook the onions and garlic gently for at least 15 minutes. Add the remaining spice mix and stir.
- Add the carrots and cook until softening, then add the sausages and chicken. Tip in the chickpeas and increase the heat to brown.
- Add the tomatoes, stock and dates with the honey and season. Cover with a lid and bake in the oven for 1 hour.
- Meanwhile soak the couscous in the boiling stock covered with cling film for 5 minutes. Remove and separate the grains with a fork.
- When the chicken is cooked, season. Serve with the cous cous.

Chicken with Wild Rice   ### 573

- Replace the couscous with cooked wild rice.

574
SERVES 4

Creole Chicken Coconut Curry

PREPARATION TIME 15 MINUTES
COOKING TIME 30 MINUTES

....

INGREDIENTS

2 tbsp olive oil
4 chicken drumsticks
1 onion, peeled and chopped
1 green pepper, seeded
and chopped
1 stick celery, finely chopped
2 cloves of garlic, finely chopped
1 cm (½ in) piece fresh ginger, finely
chopped
4 tomatoes, cored and diced
1 tbsp flour
1 tsp paprika
1 tsp Cayenne pepper
400 g / 14 oz / 1 ½ cups coconut milk
100 ml / 3 ½ fl. oz / ½ cup chicken
stock
1 bay leaf
salt and pepper
1 bunch spring onions (scallions),
finely sliced lengthways

- Heat the oil in a large pan and cook the drumsticks on all sides until golden then remove and set aside. Sauté the onion, peppers and celery until softened.
- Add the garlic, ginger and flour and cook out for a few seconds, then add the chicken back to the pan with the tomatoes.
- Sprinkle over the spices, then pour in coconut milk and stock. Add the bay leaf and season, then simmer for about 20 minutes over a low heat until the sauce has thickened and the chicken is cooked.
- Serve decorated with the spring onions

Light Creole Curry   ### 575

- Use the same amount of canned tomatoes as coconut milk for a fresher dish.

Index

Index

Chicken, Apple and Peanut Skewers 36

Chicken, Cheese and Spinach Muffins 27

Chicken, Cheese and Sun-dried Tomato Fondants 26

Chicken, Chestnut, Prune and Fig Tagine 124

Chicken, Chickpea and Asparagus Salad 41

Chicken, Corn and Vegetable Rice 88

Chicken, Courgette and Walnut Crumble 73

Chicken, Feta and Beetroot Salad 100

Chicken, Fig and Mange Tout Salad 54

Chicken, Ham and Apple Bagel 34

Chicken, Lemon and Olive Fricassee 107

Chicken, Orange and Pepper Kebabs 48

Chicken, Pepper and Bacon Tagine 86

Chicken, Potato and Mushroom Pie 113

Chicken, Raisin and Almond Salad 60

Chicken, Swede and Mushroom Pie 113

Chicken, Sweet Potato and Grape Stew 139

Chilli Chicken Noodles 137

Chilli Chicken with Ratatouille 140

Chilli Lemon Chicken 124

Chilli Orange Chicken 124

Chinese Chicken and Vegetables with Rice 132

Chinese Chicken Baguettes 85

Chinese Chicken Stir-fry 85

Chinese Chicken with Noodles 140

Chinese Flavoured Pâté 13

Chinese-style Chicken 155

Cider Chicken with Apples 79

Citrus Chicken with Sesame Seeds 28

Coconut Milk Chicken Soup 169

Colombo Style Chicken Legs 12

Colombo Style Chicken Wings 12

Creamy Chicken 65

Creamy Chicken Crumble 159

Creamy Chicken Lasagne 107

Creamy Chicken Soup 25

Creamy Chicken with Crème Fraîche 65

Creamy Chicken with Rice 163

Creamy Cider Chicken 79

Creamy Indian Curry 123

Creamy Paprika Chicken 131

Creole Chicken Coconut Curry 172

Crispy Chicken Muffins 89

Crispy Chicken Nuggets 23

Crispy Chicken with Cherry Soup 40

Crispy Chicken with Sweet Potato Mash 87

Crunchy Asian Chicken Salad 110

Crunchy Chicken and Fig Salad 54

Crunchy Chicken Carrot Cake 33

Crunchy Chicken Wings with Asparagus 30

Curried Chicken Kebabs 52

Curried Chicken Sandwich 29

Dumplings with Chinese Dipping Sauce 90

Etouffee with Spring Vegetables 65

Exotic Chicken Salad 51

Exotic Salad with Mango 51

Fajitas with Avocado and Tomato Salsa 114

Festival Tequila Chicken 31

Fragrant Chicken Parcels 79

Fricassee Sandwiches 126

Fried Chicken with Dipping Sauce 100

Fruity Chicken Curry 146

Fruity Indian Chicken Curry 123

Fruity Roast Chicken 94

Fruity Roast Chicken with Rice 94

Ginger Chicken with Crunchy Vegetables 130

Gingerbread and Port Chicken 133

Glazed Chicken Wings 18

Grated Courgette Salad 139

Green Peppercorn Chicken and Rice 128

Gremolata 154

Griddled Chicken with Aioli 14

Griddled Chicken with Farfalle & Artichokes 69

Griddled Chicken with Farfalle 69

Griddled Chicken with Lime 166

Grilled Chicken and Halloumi Skewers 113

Grilled Chicken and Spring Vegetables 59

Grilled Chicken and Tofu Skewers 113

Grilled Chicken with Bananas and Lime Rice 99

Grilled Chicken with Hot Peppercorn Sauce 37

Grilled Chicken with Paprika 140

Grilled Honey Mustard Chicken 104

Grilled Kebabs 102

Grilled Mustard Chicken Legs 104

Grilled Pepper Chicken 37

Grilled Spicy Chicken in Lemon Leaves 166

Guinea Fowl with Bacon Stuffing 110

Guinea Fowl with Chanterelle Stuffing 110

Herby Baked Chicken 97

Herby Chicken and Potato Salad 93

Herby Chicken Couscous 120

Herby Chicken Nuggets 23

Herby Chicken Salad 93

Honey and Mustard Chicken with Polenta 39

Honey Lime Chicken 98

Honey Lime Chicken Kebabs 98

Honey Mustard Chicken with Croutons 39

Honey Mustard Chicken with Noodles 39

Imperial Chicken 155

Indian Chicken and Potato Frittata 93

Indian Chicken Burgers 95

Indian Chicken Curry 123

Indian Chicken Frittata 93

Indian Chicken Soup 142

Indian Lentil Chicken Soup 153

Indian Sesame Skewers 37

Indian-marinated Chicken 122

Jambalaya Chicken and Prawns 163

Japanese Fried Chicken 100

Jerk Chicken with Okra 153

Jerk Chicken Wraps 153

Jewelled Bollywood Soup 43

Kentucky Corn Chicken 26

Kentucky Polenta Chicken 26

Kicking Chicken Wings 30

Lavender Chicken 15

Lemon and Chervil Chicken 78

Lemon Chicken Rice Paper Rolls 53

Lemon Chicken Salad 20

Lemon Chicken with Cantonese Rice 82

Lemon Ginger Chicken 82

Lemony Chicken with Fennel 96

Light Chicken Cannelloni 115

Light Chicken Salad 34

Light Creole Curry 172

Lime Chicken with Vegetable Rosette 98

Marinated Chicken Brochettes 22

Meatballs with Courgette 46

Meatballs with Hummus 46

Meaty Basque Chicken 80

Mediterranean Chicken 75

Mediterranean Chicken Tart 112

Mediterranean Tray-bake 87

Mexican-style Chicken Hash 150

Mini Chicken and Pea Pies 68

Mini Chicken Liver Terrines 55

Mini Chicken Meatballs 84

Minted Chicken Tikka 120

Moroccan Chicken Couscous 120

Moroccan Chicken with Couscous 170

Mozzarella Chicken and Vegetable Tart 112

Oat-crusted Chicken Bites 41

Index